practice
mix
perfect

How to become a Thermomix pro

Sophia Handschuh

www.thermomixbakingblogger.com

Thank you to my lovely parents and wonderful partner Jesse
for being so supportive and giving me the chance to follow my dreams.

First published in Great Britain in 2016 by Sophia Handschuh
This edition published in 2017
Enquiries: admin@thermomixbakingblogger.com
www.thermomixbakingblogger.com

contents

'Practice makes perfect'

....

....

introduction

'Everything is hard before it is easy'

I still remember the first day I got my Thermomix. After fiddling with all the settings, I finally figured out how to knead bread dough and I have never looked back. There have been many occasions of mashed onions, flat egg whites and a dough that looked like anything but a future loaf of bread. All I can say though is practice makes perfect, or 'practice mix perfect' as the title of the book suggests. When you use your Thermi, you will almost certainly discover a new trick every day. And isn't that such a rewarding feeling when you have come a step closer to ultimate kitchen efficiency? From raw food all the way to baking, in this book you will find the top tips for Thermomixing.

I have included illustrations of the simplest tricks and best practices for using your Thermomix so that you can become a real kitchen pro. No more puréed onions and curdled buttercream; this book will teach you to think twice before you mix. Practice is the most important step to becoming a kitchen pro and you will find many delicious recipes that will guide you through your cooking journey into efficiency and fun. The most important piece of advice that I have for you is to always keep experimenting, the worst that can happen is that you end up with a smoothie. So get practicing and mix perfect. I hope you enjoy the book and will continue to use your Thermomix as much as I use mine.

my kitchen story

'Kitchen efficiency is the key to a happy life'

I often get asked how I manage to fit everything in: cooking, baking, organisation, cleaning and doing all the other tasks. When I was young, my mum taught me a very important trick: never start too many tasks at once. I have become so efficient in the kitchen because I follow this principle in all aspects of life. If you have a clear head and have a task focus, you are able to make much better decisions in the kitchen. Planning ahead is the key to that. I will cover meal planning later on in the book. My grandma, Omi, was a true kitchen pro. She organised all our meals for the entire house every day. We had our business attached to the house, so at lunch time everyone would gather and somehow she always managed to make a three course meal out of virtually nothing. She told me that the freezer is her best friend. She made use of all the seasons and always froze whatever was in season to have it ready later on. So, if you are lucky enough to live close to a lovely farmers' market, buy vegetables in season, freeze them chopped up in portions and use them later on. It will save a lot of time and effort, and will ensure you can get the best out of seasonal produce.

In my tiny kitchen in London, which is the size of a shoebox, I worship the fridge and freezer. I don't have the luxury of a big country house and freezer the size of a whole room, so I learned to be very efficient, using my Thermi and freezer to make the most of the space I have. I find that the key to kitchen efficiency is to be organised about meal planning. I always have a freezer full of meals that I prepare in advance and I can take out on a busy night. My go-to recipe is chorizo bolognese (p.112), which has a prime spot in our freezer. Because I am very keen on baking, I also prepare a few pastries to make fresh croissants on Sunday. For example, puff pastry and Danish pastry freeze very well and you can always quickly whizz up something fresh for the family without having to stand in the kitchen for hours.

I use my Thermi to make bulk tomato sauces (p.49), prepare delicious ghee (p.44) for my curries, make curry pastes to use later (p.52) and freeze some ice cream for a quick dessert (p.70). These are quick to prepare and so useful to have at home. You save money and, unlike shop bought jars of pastes, you actually know what is in them. No additives, no preservatives, just delicious ingredients. As a true omnivore I believe in eating everything in moderation, which is why I designed this book to include a bit of everything and some of my favourite cultural influences, like Indian, Mediterranean, South-East Asian and Caribbean food. You should eat whatever you are comfortable with and I welcome all diets, eating philosophies and allergies in this book to make sure everyone can share the joy of Thermi efficiency at home.

how this book works

This book is designed to help you become a Thermomix kitchen pro. It will teach you some basics if you have just bought a Thermomix and also show you how you can become even better at using your machine if you've had yours for quite a while. There are always new things you can learn and some tricks you may not have thought about, however advanced you are.

The book contains the best tips on meal planning, creating your own efficient Sunday prep night and how you can become a Thermomix pro in seven days if you are struggling to make the most of your Thermi. Each chapter has a summary of the main functions and a chopping, blending, baking, milling, etc. guide. It contains top secret tips and includes a special section within each category about one of the elements of the Thermomix. All recipes are designed to be used with both the TM5 and TM31.

the Thermi clock

I have thought about the best way to help you navigate this book and have come up with the Thermi clock. I will use the symbols for the twelve functions of the Thermomix to make it easier for you to find your way around the recipes. Having so many different elements integrated into one machine makes the Thermomix unique and you are going to learn how and when to use each function. You will see the clock symbols popping up in each recipe, guiding you through the learning process and showing you exactly when each function is used.

key to dietary labels

F	Freezable
RSF	Refined sugar free
GF	Gluten free
DF	Dairy free
V	Vegan

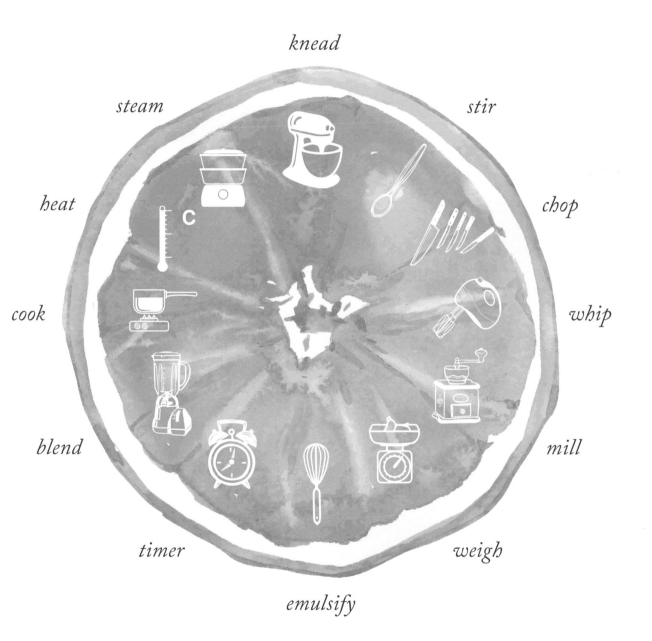

knead

steam

stir

heat

chop

cook

whip

blend

mill

timer

weigh

emulsify

weekly meal plan

Preparing your food ahead is the key to a stress-free week. Sunday night is the ideal prep night and means that no matter how tired you are in the week, you will always have some food in the fridge that you can whizz up quickly. Cook your vegetables, grains, pulses and pasta ahead and make yourself a few dips, salad dressings and a loaf of bread on Sunday. This section will show you how to make a meal plan, teach you the importance of a shopping list and give you a guide for Sunday prep night.

make a weekly plan

I usually sit down with a cup of tea on a Friday afternoon and make my weekly meal plan. I put that appointment in my diary as if I am going on a date with my boyfriend. When you make your weekly plan, make sure to include all meals, including breakfast, lunch, snacks, dinner and any baking. You can always plan the meals so that you can use the leftovers from dinner for the next day's lunch. In the online shop on my blog you can find a complete kit for meal planning.

To make the meal plan, start by listing all the dinners including vegetables, meat/fish/beans, grains/pulses/pasta and a sauce. Then move onto the lunches, using any leftovers from the previous night's dinner. Make sure to prepare a lunch for Monday because you won't have any leftovers yet. Finally, plan some snacks and breakfasts for the week. Overnight oats, which is on p.62 is a great bulk breakfast.

the importance of a shopping list

Once your weekly meal plan is done, you need to make a shopping list. Since I started making a meal plan and going shopping with a purpose, I have saved so much money and reduced my food waste considerably. Remember never to go shopping hungry! It is fatal to your pocket and you will see things land in your shopping basket that you never thought you needed before. Use the weekly meal planner day by day to make your shopping list. Go through each recipe and think about exactly what you need and write it down. My shopping day is Saturday morning so that I have everything for Sunday prep night ready and I can enjoy my weekend.

Sunday prep night

On Sunday night, after you have had a great weekend, start your weekly meal prep. This is the last step to efficient weekly meal planning. If you have kids, get them involved so that they learn about food preparation, cooking and just simply have some fun. Start by steaming all your veggies, except for green veggies, in the Varoma. This may have to be done in batches. While you do that, cook your grains/pulses in the simmering basket. You can find the guide to cooking these ingredients on p.89. You can also cook all the meats for the week in the Varoma/simmering basket and freeze in portions. Soups, stews or sauces can be made in larger batches and frozen in single portions. Bake your perfect bloomer loaf (p.130) and prepare some dips and dressings. For breakfast you can pre-boil eggs in the simmering basket for 15 minutes, place under cold water and store in the fridge for up to seven days. Make your overnight oats every three days and also store these in the fridge.

Sunday prep night

Sunday prep night can be organised very efficiently so that you don't end up spending your entire Sunday preparing food for the whole week. Get the kids or your partner involved and get started. I have included an example of a weekly planner, a summary of elements for a dinner and a Sunday prep night checklist so that you have a great guide to start with.

The weekly planner example below takes into account both healthy and naughty meals, snacks and breakfasts, and uses leftovers from dinner for next-day lunches. It will help you determine how you can plan your weekly meals. You can find most of the recipes for this weekly meal plan in this book. Use the layout of this plan as inspiration for all your weekly planning. Make sure to also include a day for going out for dinner with friends or your partner. You deserve a break once in a while.

	Breakfast	*Lunch*	*Snacks/Baking*	*Dinner*
M	Overnight oats with raspberries (p.62)	Raw detox salad (p.76)	Raw beetroot balls (p.66)	Chorizo bolognese (p.112)
T	Chocolate overnight oats (p.62)	Leftover bolognese on jacket potato	Parmesan rosemary shortbread (p.142)	Pizza fakeout (p.140)
W	Smashed avocado eggs on toast (p.98)	Mini pizza bites with salad	Fro-yo bites (p.70)	Jerk chicken (p.110)
T	Poppyseed bloomer loaf (p.130) with notella (p.28)	Jerk chicken salad	Blueberry cookies (p.146)	Coconut dal (p.104) with pitta bread (p.136)
F	Key lime smoothie (p.68)	Coconut dal with rice	Nutty snacks (p.36)	Beetroot burgers (p.103)
S	Berry scones (p.145) with raspberry curd (p.33)	Beetroot crumbles with rocket salad	Salted caramel fudge (p.34)	Roast beef with celeriac mash (p.114)
S	Quinoa chia bread (p.134) with homemade ricotta (p.41)	Roast beef sandwiches	Mini victoria sponges (p.148)	Thai prawn soup (p.109)

Sunday Prep Night Checklist

Cooking / portion freezing meat

Cooking grains / pulses / pasta

Pre-boiling eggs

Preparing snacks

Making salad dressings

Preparing dips

Making breakfast

Baking breads

Steaming vegetables

Thermomix pro challenge

Are you struggling to integrate Thermomix into your cooking routine? Does it seem daunting and like a lot of effort? Well, you should give this handy seven-day programme to becoming a Thermomix pro a try. Every day you are encouraged to try out a few functions and come a step closer to being the ultimate kitchen pro. It is not all that hard, just remember to experiment lots, use it every day and don't worry about failing.

Day 1:

We will start with a few very simple, yet rewarding tasks. Your blade is very powerful, so be careful never to use too high a speed, otherwise you may end up with mashed onions or blended salad. Today, you will learn to chop vegetables and onions, and make a raw and tasty salad. Find the recipe for this on p.76

Day 2:

Well done for making a start. You have already got to know your powerful Thermomix blade. Today, you will learn how to make a soup. A really delicious recipe that teaches you the blending and combining functions is a delicious roasted cauliflower soup with chickpeas on p.106.

Day 3:

After having made a successful soup and a really tasty salad, let's cook something for dinner. How about a family classic: spaghetti bolognese. My absolute favourite is a little twist to the classic: chorizo bolognese (p.112). You can easily freeze the leftover sauce afterwards in individual portions.

Day 4:

You are already approaching a new level of cooking and becoming so efficient it will make your friends jealous. You know how to make your favourite family dinner and how to prepare great starters and sides. Let's learn how to make one of those famous all-in-one meals. The ultimate roast beef recipe will guide you through on p.114, and you will also learn about the Varoma.

Day 5:

Enough cooking for one week. Let's get baking. Your first cake, a marble crumble cake, will be a great success. Don't worry, it will be super tasty, fluffy and exactly what you need to celebrate your achievements. Follow the recipe on p.151.

Day 6:

You deserve a bit of an easy one today. After all that hard work, get the kids or your partner involved and let them help. It's pizza night and you will learn how to make your very own dough from scratch on p.140.

Day 7:

Congratulations, you have done an incredible job in the last six days, so pat yourself on the back. Time to get sophisticated. Your last task is my favourite: making bread from scratch. Bread is so simple, just follow the instructions very carefully and remember, if the dough is not as you wish, just try it again. You can find a tasty recipe for a fluffy poppyseed bloomer loaf on p.130.

ingredients & equipment

When you are cooking and baking the recipes in this book, it helps to have a quick look at some of the common ingredients I use so that you can make sure that you have the right sized eggs, know when your avocados are ripe and what type of flour to use. If you are struggling to get hold of any equipment, it is worth checking my online shop; you will be able to find most of the equipment you need there.

Agave Nectar	Agave nectar is a great sweetener that you can use instead of honey or sugar. I use it in quite a few recipes.
Avocados	Avocados are perfect for many things other than cooking. I use them to make ice cream and desserts, and for breakfast. You can check whether an avocado is ripe by gently pressing it. If it yields, it is ripe. If it feels very firm, then leave it to ripen a bit longer.
Beetroot	You can use beetroot both raw and cooked. When raw, it serves as a great ingredient for making snacks and salads. When cooked, you can use it as a side dish for any meal. When you boil beetroot, make sure it is unpeeled, otherwise it will lose its colour.
Butter	For all recipes I use unsalted butter unless otherwise stated in the recipe.
Chia Seeds	Chia seeds are very good as a thickening agent and as part of a dessert. They are also perfect for breakfast. Please note, chia seeds expand when they come into contact with water so you can soak 1 tsp chia seeds in 3 tsp water and leave for 15 minutes and use as a replacement for 1 egg.
Double Cream	Double cream is usually used in recipes to thicken sauces or to make ganache. This may be called heavy cream or thick cream in other countries.
Eggs	I use large eggs for everything when baking and cooking. I find they are the ideal size to achieve fluffy cakes.
Flour Types	For all breads I use strong white bread flour. For all other bakes, such as cakes and scones, I use plain flour.
Milk	I only use whole milk for my recipes. It gives a better and more wholesome flavour.
Nut Butter	When a recipe states to use nut butter, you can use any nut butter you like. It is up to you whether it is crunchy or smooth.
Nut Milk	I make my own nut milk (p.38) but you can also use any nut milk you like for the recipes in this book.

1-Pound or 2-Pound Loaf Tin	The 1- and 2-pound loaf tins are perfect for making bread.
18cm, 20cm, 22cm Round Springform Cake Tin	Springform cake tins are my favourite. I use different sized cake tins, but most commonly I use the 20cm cake tin because I love layering the sponges to make a cake with height.
23cm Flan Tin or Fluted Pie Tin	I have two different types of pastry tins: one is fluted and one is flat. It does not matter which one you use, but one with a loose bottom is the best.
Bread Proofing Basket	A bread proofing basket is the perfect way to shape your bread. I recommend using a real Banneton basket and keeping it floured.
Dough Scraper	The dough scraper is vital to breadmaking. You can use it to cut dough or clean up the work surface later on.
Greaseproof Paper	The greaseproof paper I use is non-stick and perfect for all baking.
Ice Cube Trays	Ice cube trays are perfect for freezing bite-sized ice creams, veggie stock cubes and spice pastes.
Mason Jars	Mason jars exist in many different sizes and are perfect for storing. I recommend ones made by Weck.
Muslin Cloth or Nut milk Bag	I use a muslin cloth or nut milk bag to strain my cheese, nut milk and butter.
Rectangular Baking Tray	I use the same size rectangular baking tray for most of my recipes. Just make sure it fits inside your oven and you will be fine.
Rolling Pin	A rolling pin is a must when rolling out cookies, scones or any other pastry. I prefer a wooden rolling pin because it grabs flour better.
Square Baking Tin	I use a 20cm x 20cm square baking tin for most of my recipes. If you have a larger one, make sure to divide it using a piece of aluminium foil rolled tightly like a tube.
Varoma Liners	Instead of using greaseproof paper to line your Varoma you can also use ready cut Varoma liners.

freezing guide

'The big chill'

In this book you will learn how to be a Thermomix pro with as little effort as possible. I know how busy all our lives are and it is nearly impossible for some of us to juggle motherhood, jobs and being able to cook a healthy and wholesome meal and still find time to spend with our families. Luckily, this book is designed to give you freezing advice for most of the recipes. This handy freezer guide helps you determine how to freeze and teaches you the dos and don'ts of freezing.

freezing preparation

When you are preparing food for freezing, make sure only to use packaging materials that are airtight and water resistant so that you maintain the best quality of your food. I usually label the packaging with the date I have frozen it so that I know roughly when I need to eat it by. Food in large containers freezes too slowly, so make sure to use smaller containers or portion sized bags.

Do use: Plastic freezer containers, plastic freezer bags, aluminium foil, foil trays, cling film, heavy plastic wrap, zip-lock bags.

Do not use: Glass jars, cottage cheese or yoghurt containers, sandwich bags, wax paper.

best not to freeze

Just because you can put almost any food in the freezer does not mean that you should. There are a few things that are not suitable for freezing, and below is a list of the ones that are a no-go. You don't want to compromise the quality of the food, so avoid freezing any of the below.

Cheese in blocks	Crumbles and loses taste
Custards	Becomes watery
Cooked eggs, cooked egg whites and raw yolks	Becomes rubbery, crumbly and gummy
Lettuce	Becomes watery and flat
Tomatoes	Become watery and limp
Dairy products, such as milk, yogurt, mayonnaise	Some separation can occur
Potatoes, raw	May darken

what to freeze

Below you will find the best practice for freezing some of the food that you can cook in this book.

Freshly baked bread & bread rolls	Freeze after you have baked the bread rolls or loaf of bread in individual freezer bags. Thaw, then bake again for 5 minutes at 200°C. To freeze bread rolls raw, make sure the dough balls are not in contact with each other. Bake from frozen for 20 minutes at 200°C.
Shortcrust pastry	You can easily freeze shortcrust pastry by either wrapping it in cling film or in a freezer bag. Thaw in the fridge overnight or at room temperature before using.
Biscuits & cookies	Baked cookies and biscuits can be frozen in individual portioned freezer bags. Thaw, then bake for 5 minutes at 180°C to refresh.
Rough puff or filo pastry	Using a rolling pin, roll out your pastry first before freezing. Place on a piece of grease-proof paper and roll up, then freeze covered with cling film. Thaw before needed. You can also freeze it as a block, but make sure to defrost it in the fridge before using.
Pizza bases (raw)	Roll out your pizza base into the shape you want. It can either be rectangular to fit an oven tray or round for a pizza tray. Wrap in a large freezer bag and freeze. Thaw before continuing with the topping and baking.
Pizza (baked)	When you are freezing baked pizza, make sure to take it out of the oven 2 minutes before it is baked. Freeze covered in cling film and bake from frozen for 15 minutes at 220°C.
Chopped onions	Place 2 peeled and halved onions in the mixing bowl and chop **3 Sec. / Speed 5**. Place into small freezer containers and freeze until you need them again. You can scoop out individual portions whenever you need onions and just add a couple of minutes' frying time to allow for proper defrosting while cooking.
Jams	You can freeze jams by pouring them into a plastic freezer container. Do not attempt to freeze in jars as they might break. Thaw before using again.

Butter	Butter can be frozen in two ways. Either place the butter into a plastic freezer container or roll up in cling film and cut into individual portions. Thaw as needed.
Sauces, soups, stews & curries	Pour the cooled sauce, soup, stew or curry into individual freezer bags or plastic freezer containers. It is always best to do this in portions rather than one big batch of sauce as it will freeze better. Thaw before reheating.
Minced meat	Mince whole beef chuck or pork shoulder in the mixing bowl first (see guide on p.57) then place into individual freezer bags and thaw before using.
Sponge cakes	You can easily freeze a baked sponge cake. Wrap the cooled cake in a double layer of cling film and a single layer of aluminium foil. Thaw for about 4–6 hours before using.
Cheesecakes	Place any moist cake on a ceramic serving plate or the bottom of the springform tin you used for baking the cake and wrap in cling film. Leave any toppings, such as fruit, off and decorate after thawing. Thaw in the fridge before serving. On a very hot day, you can also serve the cheesecake as a cheesecake ice cream cake.
Vegetables	Chop vegetables into small chunks, then steam in the Varoma, adding 900g water to the mixing bowl **5 Min. / Varoma / Speed 1**. Tip into the simmering basket and pour ice cold water over them to stop the cooking process. Pour into individual portioned freezer bags and freeze. Thaw before using.
Fruit	Chop fruit into small chunks, then freeze in individually portioned freezer bags.
Cooked meats	Slice up your cooked meat, such as roast beef or pork shoulder, and shred your chicken first. Then place into plastic freezer containers or freezer bags and freeze. Thaw before using.

thawing

There are several methods for safe thawing. If you live in a hot country or the weather is particularly hot, place the frozen food in the fridge and leave to thaw overnight. The fridge method is the slowest and safest option. For a quicker method you can also place the frozen food in a waterproof bag and submerge in tepid water but you have to cook it immediately after thawing.

If you need even quicker results, place the frozen food in a microwaveable container and thaw on the defrost setting of the microwave. Check every 10 minutes and scrape off any thawed food. Please note that any method except for the fridge method is not suitable for re-freezing.

how long to freeze

When properly stored, all frozen foods are safe forever, but they do lose taste at some point, so always make sure to use the oldest packs of frozen food first and follow these maximum storage recommendations for frozen foods.

	1 Month	2 Months	3 Months	6 Months	9 Months	12 Months
Meats		Smoked or cured meats (e.g. bacon, sausages, etc.)	Cooked meats	Ground meats (e.g. mince, burger patties)		Beef, pork, lamb or veal (e.g. chops, roasts and steaks)
Poultry		Chicken or turkey breast	Shredded chicken	Ground poultry (e.g. patties, mince) fried chicken, rotisserie chicken		Chicken, turkey or goose whole or in pieces
Seafood			Fatty fish (e.g. salmon, mackerel)	Shellfish (e.g. mussels, clams, crab meat, lobster, shrimps)	Lean fish (e.g. cod, haddock, sole)	
Sauces, soups, curries & stews				All soups, sauces, stews and curries in individual portions		
Dairy			Milk and buttermilk	Ice cream		Butter
Baked goods		Pies and quiches	Cakes, cheesecakes, bread rolls, loaves of bread, bagels and tortillas			Cookies and biscuits
Vegetables and fruit	Bananas, grapes, melon	Tofu	Berries	Vegetables		Tempeh, soy meat substitutes

In this chapter I will show you the best tricks and recipes for those pantry essentials you usually buy in the supermarket. Prepare for delicious 'Notella' and beautifully homemade flavoured butters.

....

essentials

the Thermomix mindset

'Ready, set, reverse'

Before you start with any of the wonderful tips, tasks and recipes in the book, you need to enter the Thermomix mindset. Below you will find my top rules for using Thermomix. They will help you become a much better chef and understand exactly what to do wherever you are in your cooking career.

think in reverse

When you work with a recipe which is not Thermomix converted, it is important to work backwards. Once you have set your mind to reverse mode, it will be easier to understand how to use your Thermomix. Always look at a recipe first and think about how long each ingredient takes to cook. For example, start with the rice, then attach the Varoma and steam hard veggies first, then soft ones, then fish or chicken.

dry first, then wet

Dry ingredients need to be prepared before beginning the recipe to avoid longer cleaning times. For example, grind the nuts first, mill the flour first, make the icing sugar first, then move on to the next steps in the recipe.

caution on higher speeds

To avoid puréed onions and mashed veggies, use these guides for chopping and blitzing with Thermomix.

- **< Speed 5**: roughly chopped, combining cake batter
- **Speeds 5–7**: finely chopped, grating cheese
- **Speeds 8–10**: blending, puréeing soup, grinding spices, milling flour

recipe language

Reading recipes made for the Thermomix is slightly different to standard recipes. Every recipe always includes Time / Temperature / Speed so that you can just dial in the right numbers and go. This is the standard format in which a recipe is displayed.

TM5 to TM31

This book is primarily designed to work for TM5; however, you can easily use it with the TM31 as well. Make sure, however, you convert recipes bearing the maximum bowl capacity in mind. For example, any soups, sauces or chopping large amounts of vegetables may need to be done in two batches as the mixing bowl capacity is only 2l in the TM31 compared to 2.2l in the TM5.

basic Thermi tips

1   When pouring liquids into the bowl, you can put the measuring cup in place and pour the liquid around it onto the lid to let it drop down slowly. This is especially helpful when you are squeezing lemon juice and want to catch any pips or when making mayonnaise and want to pour in the oil slowly. The measuring cup prevents the liquid from dropping down too quickly and creates a gentle stream.

2   When you are grinding small amounts of ingredients, insert the simmering basket so that you avoid having, for example, whole spices being dispersed too far.

3   Use your spatula to cut through any dough and divide it into individual pieces. It is the perfect tool for scoring bread rolls and scraping dough off the work surface as well.

4   Your measuring cup can measure liquids of up to 100g. This does not apply to oils or thicker liquids. Either you can measure it to the halfway point, which equals 50g, or the full point, which is 100g. This is the same for both the TM5 and TM31.

5   When you are working with heavy cake batters, lots of veggies, tough pastes or dips, insert the spatula through the lid and swirl around to help achieve a smoother consistency. The spatula is designed not to touch the blade.

6   Once you have removed a dough from the mixing bowl, use the turbo function to whack any dough residue against the mixing bowl and separate it from the blade. It makes cleaning your bowl much easier.

7   Make sure to turn your spatula clockwise in the bowl to remove anything, otherwise you may end up with some nasty looking nicks in the spatula. Going clockwise means avoiding the sharp side of the blade.

8   If you are weighing any ingredients for later use, place a bowl on top of the mixing bowl lid and start the weighing function. Press tare and add in the ingredients you want. Then you can easily remove the bowl from the lid and place it aside for later use, allowing you to weigh your ingredients without having to take out your kitchen scales.

9   When you are chopping anything that is quite hard, such as large vegetable pieces, only fill up the mixing bowl halfway so that everything can be chopped up to the same size. Filling up your mixing bowl too much will cause some veggies to stay large while others get chopped too finely.

10   There are two ways to sterilise your jars. You can either place them in the sink and boil some water in a kettle. Once boiled, carefully pour the water over the jars and leave to cool slightly in the sink before rinsing. This can be dangerous so keep children away and exercise caution when pouring the boiling water into the sink. Alternatively, you can place the jars in the Varoma. Fill the mixing bowl with 1000g water and put the Varoma in place. Cook **15 Min. / Varoma / Speed 1**. Carefully remove the jars using oven gloves and leave to cool before filling.

notella

There is a special technique to opening chocolate hazelnut spread. The key is to crack open the golden lining with a knife, then pull it back and have just one spoonful immediately. Such a lovely treat. But also packed with calories, sugar and preservatives. Because I have liked chocolate hazelnut spread since I was a child, I have developed this vegan version with no refined sugar and a slightly different technique to standard nut butter making. I call it 'Notella'. It is perfect for the kids and lasts really well in the fridge for up to four weeks.

makes
1 jar

150g hazelnuts
6 dates, pitted
40g cocoa powder

200g maple syrup
120g almond milk (p.38)
1 Tbsp vanilla extract

1. Preheat the oven to 200°C / 180°C Fan / Gas Mark 6.
2. Place the hazelnuts on a large rectangular tray lined with greaseproof paper and roast for 10 minutes. Leave to cool, then tip into the mixing bowl.
3. Add the dates, cocoa powder, maple syrup, almond milk and vanilla extract and blitz **1.5 Min. / Speed 10**.
4. Pour into a sterilised jar (you can read about sterilising a jar in the beginning of this chapter) and keep in the fridge for up to 4 weeks.

I will learn: How to use the blending function to make super smooth nut spread in less than 2 minutes

V GF DF F

strawberrylicious jam

Strawberry jam is one of my all-time favourites. When the strawberry season was in full bloom, my mum and I would always go out and pick some fresh strawberries from the fields. Our hands were completely red and our faces also looked the part. At home, we made strawberry jam and it was always so delicious. I have recreated my mum's original because she used a lot less sugar and instead used chia seeds to make it thick. Less sugar, more flavour.

makes
1 jar

150g rhubarb
200g raspberries
250g strawberries
350g jam sugar

3 tsp chia seeds
1 vanilla pod
¼ tsp citric acid

1. Start by chopping the rhubarb into small chunks and removing the stalks from the straw-berries. Place the strawberries in the mixing bowl along with the raspberries, jam sugar, chia seeds and citric acid. Chop **15 Sec. / Speed 5**.
2. Add the vanilla pod and cook **15 Min. / 100°C / Reverse / Speed 2**.
3. Test whether the jam is cooked by pouring a teaspoon of the jam onto a plate. Leave to cool and if you run through the jam with the edge of a spoon and the gap remains, the jam is done.
4. If you prefer smooth jam, strain the jam through the simmering basket into a pourable jug and then pour into sterilized jam jars (you can read about sterilising a jar at the beginning of this chapter) and seal tight. Refrigerate for up to 1 month.

I will learn: How to make incredibly tasty and smooth jam using the cook function and passing it through the simmering basket

colourful curds

Curds are a special treat for any time of the day. Whether eaten for breakfast on a freshly toasted piece of bread or on top of a cake to create a zingy taste, here are two versions that can be used in the most amazing ways. Try the passionfruit curd on a Victoria sponge cake (p.148) or the raspberry curd with some mascarpone and fresh raspberries as a dessert. Gorgeous colours and beautifully smooth texture.

raspberry curd

makes
1 jar

240g sugar
2 limes, zest only
120g butter

3 eggs
100g lime juice
100g raspberries

1. Place the sugar in the mixing bowl. Mill **15 Sec. / Speed 10**. Add the lime zest and mill again **20 Sec. / Speed 10**.
2. Add the butter, eggs, lime juice and raspberries to the mixing bowl. Cook **20 Min. / 90°C / Speed 2 / no measuring cup**.
3. Once cooked, place the measuring cup on the lid and blend **25 Sec. / Speed 6**.
4. Pour into two sterilised jars (you can read about sterilising a jar at the beginning of this chapter) and seal tight. Store in the fridge for up to 1 month.

passionfruit curd

makes
1 jar

240g sugar
2 lemons, zest and juice
120g butter

3 eggs
150g passionfruit flesh

1. Place the sugar in the mixing bowl. Mill **15 Sec. / Speed 10**. Add the lemon zest and mill again **20 Sec. / Speed 10**.
2. Add the butter, eggs, lemon juice and passionfruit flesh to the mixing bowl. Cook **20 Min. / 90°C / Speed 2 / no measuring cup**.
3. Once cooked, place the measuring cup on the lid and blend **25 Sec. / Speed 6**.
4. Pour into two sterilised jars (you can read about sterilising a jar at the beginning of this chapter) and seal tight. Store in the fridge for up to 1 month.

GF F

salted caramel fudge

If you have ever had the pleasure of eating fudge, you probably know why adding the words 'salted caramel' to it can only mean one thing: addiction alert. Oh, and yes, you are able to make fudge in your Thermomix. With this recipe you can learn to make the creamiest and most perfect fudge, and it will not last on the kitchen counter for long. Warning: may cause serious happiness. Instead of salt, you can also sprinkle with freeze-dried fruit if you like.

makes
16–20

200g white chocolate, in small chunks
1 can (395g) condensed milk
125g butter

160g brown sugar
125g golden syrup
½ tsp sea salt flakes

1. Place the white chocolate in the mixing bowl. Blitz **5 Sec. / Speed 9**. Pour into a separate bowl until later.
2. Add the condensed milk, butter, brown sugar and golden syrup to the mixing bowl. Cook again **28 Min. / Varoma / Speed 3 / no measuring cup**.
3. Meanwhile, line a 15–20cm square tin with cling film.
4. Add the chopped white chocolate to the mixing bowl and mix **20 Sec. / Speed 4**.
5. Pour into the prepared tin, sprinkle with the sea salt and leave to set for at least 4 hours. Alternatively, you can refrigerate for 2 hours instead.
6. Once set, remove from the tin and place on a chopping board. If the fudge does not come out easily, leave it to come to room temperature for a few minutes first. Chop up into bite-sized chunks. You can keep the fudge in a jar for up to 1 month.

I will learn: How to heat without the measuring cup in the lid to reduce liquids

nutty snacks

These super nutty snacks are perfect for in between meals. Whether you are craving sweet, roasted almonds or turmeric spiced cashew nuts, always have some with you on the go. They can be stored in a jar for up to 1 month.

roasted almonds

makes
1 jar

200g almonds, skin on
80g brown sugar
1 pinch of cinnamon

½ teaspoon vanilla extract
10g water

1. Preheat the oven to 180°C / 160°C Fan / Gas Mark 4. Line a large rectangular tray with grease-proof paper.
2. Place the almonds, brown sugar, cinnamon and vanilla extract in the mixing bowl. Roast 6 Min. / Varoma / Reverse / Speed 1.
3. Add the water and roast again 3 Min. / Varoma / Reverse / Speed 1 / no measuring cup. If the almonds are starting to look dry, add a little more water.
4. Pour the almonds onto the prepared tray and roast in the oven for 10–15 minutes.

turmeric cashews

makes
1 jar

200g cashews
½ tsp sea salt
½ tsp ground turmeric

½ tsp cayenne pepper
1 Tbsp sesame seeds
10g water

1. Preheat the oven to 180°C. Line a large rectangular tray with greaseproof paper.
2. Place the cashews, sea salt, ground turmeric, cayenne pepper and sesame seeds in the mixing bowl. Roast 4 Min. / Varoma / Reverse Speed 1.
3. Add the water and roast again 2 Min. / Varoma / Reverse / Speed 1 / no measuring cup.
4. Pour the cashews onto the prepared tray and roast in the oven for 10–15 minutes.

I will learn: How to caramelise using the Thermomix instead of having to watch your saucepan at all times

go nuts for milk

There is not much that tops the taste of homemade nut milk. If you are lactose intolerant or if you just don't like the taste of cow's milk, this is one of the best alternatives to try at home. The simmering basket is used in all parts of this recipe to rinse, strain and pour and is a great little helper for the nut milk making process.

cashew or almond milk

makes
0.75l

200g cashews or almonds
1000g cold water + extra for soaking
1 tsp honey (optional)

1. Start by soaking the nuts in water. Place a large bowl on top of the mixing bowl lid and weigh them in. Fill the bowl with cold water so that the nuts are completely covered and leave to soak for 4–5 hours.
2. Rinse the nuts well by pouring them into the simmering basket and running some cold water over them. Then transfer the nuts into the mixing bowl and pour over the water. Add the honey and blitz 1 Min. / Speed 10.
3. Place a muslin cloth or a nut milk bag in the simmering basket. Pour the milk mixture over the cloth and strain into a bowl. Catch the milk and discard the leftover nuts.

cashew cream

makes
0.75l

50g cashews
100g water + extra for soaking
30g vegetable oil

1. Start by soaking the nuts in water. Place a large bowl on top of the Thermomix lid and weigh them in. Fill the bowl with cold water so that the nuts are completely covered and leave to soak for 4–5 hours.
2. Rinse the nuts well by pouring them into the simmering basket and running some cold water over them. Then transfer the nuts into the mixing bowl and pour over the water and vegetable oil. Blitz 1 Min. / Speed 10. Serve alongside cake, as part of sauces or as the base for ice cream.

I will learn: — The best way to use your simmering basket for rinsing, straining and pouring
— How to use the blending function, scale and timer

chocolate hazelnut milk

makes
0.75l

200g roasted hazelnuts
900g water + extra for soaking
5 dates, pitted

2 Tbsp cocoa powder
1 tsp vanilla extract

1. Start by soaking the hazelnuts in water. Place a large bowl on top of the Thermomix lid and weigh in the hazelnuts. Fill the bowl with cold water so that they are completely covered and leave to soak for 4–5 hours.
2. Rinse the nuts well by pouring them into the simmering basket and running some cold water over them. Then transfer the nuts into the mixing bowl and pour over the water. Add the dates, cocoa powder and vanilla extract and blitz **1 Min. / Speed 10**.
3. Place a muslin cloth or a nut milk bag in the simmering basket. Pour the milk mixture over the cloth and strain into a bowl. Catch the milk and discard the leftover nuts.

cheese it yourself

Have you ever thought you could make your own cheese and not have to buy it again? This is one of my go-to recipes when it is Sunday night and you realise you have forgotten to buy cheese. Ricotta cheese is so easy to make, and to curdle the milk I use a special ingredient called rennet. You can usually get it in health food shops, online or from specialist stores. The vegetarian version is called VegeRen, which is what I used for this recipe.

makes
400g

2000g whole milk (non-pasteurised)
1 tsp citric acid
1 Tbsp water

1 tsp rennet
½ tsp sea salt flakes (optional)

1. Place the milk in the mixing bowl. In a small bowl, mix the citric acid with the water and pour into the mixing bowl with the milk. Warm **10 Min. / 37°C / Speed 1**.
2. Add the rennet and stir **10 Sec. / Speed 3**. Leave in the mixing bowl to curdle for 15 minutes.
3. Using a knife, make 4 horizontal lines through the curd, and then slice into 4cm squares. Leave for another 15 minutes covered with the lid and measuring cup.
4. Gently heat the cheese **40 Min. / 37°C / Speed 2**.
5. Prepare the simmering basket with a muslin cloth and place inside a large bowl. Slowly pour the mixture into the cloth and start the draining process.
6. Using your hands, squeeze as much whey out as possible. Pour the liquid into a separate container and leave the cheese in the cloth to drain for approx. 15 minutes. After that, squeeze the cloth by twisting the top until it is really tight. All the liquid should have come out by then.
7. Return the curd to the mixing bowl. Add the sea salt flakes and knead **1 Min./Kneading function**. You can use the finished Ricotta to spread on toast or crumble on salads and store in the fridge for up to 4 days.

I will learn: — How to use the gentle heat function to bring ingredients to body temperature
— How to use the kneading function to work ingredients

veggie stock cubes

Vegetable stock is one of the most basic elements in cooking. You need it for soups, sauces and even to flavour rice. It's really useful to keep handy, especially if it is already individually portioned up so you just need to take one cube out, and you have enough for 500g water. The great thing about this stock paste is that it doesn't have to be cooked and is immediately ready for freezing.

25g parmesan, in small chunks
50g carrots, in small chunks
1 celery stick, in small chunks
½ onion
1 tomato, halved
½ courgette, in small chunks
50g chestnut mushrooms
3 sundried tomatoes
20g tomato purée
¼ leek, in small chunks

3 garlic cloves
1 bay leaf
2 sprigs fresh sage
1 sprig fresh rosemary
1 sprig fresh thyme
30g fresh parsley
1 Tbsp olive oil
1 tsp black pepper
80g dry white wine
130g sea salt

1. Place the parmesan in the mixing bowl. Blitz **7 Sec. / Speed 9**. Scrape down.
2. Add the carrots, celery stick, onion, tomato, courgette, chestnut mushrooms, sundried tomatoes, tomato purée, leek, garlic cloves, bay leaf, sage, rosemary, thyme, parsley, olive oil, ground black pepper, dry white wine and sea salt. Blitz **30 Sec. / Speed 10** while stirring with spatula through hole in mixing bowl lid.
3. Pour the mixture into 3–4 ice cube trays and use your spatula to flatten it. Freeze for at least 4 hours, then use in individual portions for cooking. One cube is enough for 500g water.

Top secret tip: Don't clean the bowl after you have made this lovely stock. Fill it up with water and make some amazing vegetable broth. Cook for **20 Min. / 100°C / Speed 1** and pour into individual sterilised jars. Keep for up to 1 week in the fridge.

ghee

If you are a fan of Indian cuisine, you will have come across an ingredient called ghee. I use it for nearly every meal instead of butter. Ghee is made from butter and during the boiling process the fat completely separates from the milk solids to create this wonderfully sweet and tasty ingredient that makes onions taste a lot nicer than standard butter. It also does not burn easily when used for frying onions.

makes
1 jar

500g unsalted butter, in small chunks

1. Place the butter in the mixing bowl. Cook **45 Min. / Varoma / Speed 2**. Strain through a nut milk bag or a muslin cloth and pour into a sterilised jar (you can read about sterilising a jar at the beginning of this chapter). Store either at room temperature or in the fridge, depending on where you have more space.

wholegrain mustard

Wholegrain mustard is one of the most basic ingredients that we all buy without realising how easy it is to make at home. Whether you use it to spread over meat to create a crust or just as part of your favourite salad dressing, it is a super easy condiment to prepare. It takes so little time and effort and keeps well in the fridge for months.

makes
1 jar

150g yellow mustard seeds
150g black mustard seeds
120g cider vinegar
10g honey
1 pinch salt

1 pinch black pepper
½ tsp turmeric powder
1 pinch paprika
20g sunflower oil

1. Place the yellow and black mustard seeds in the mixing bowl. Add the cider vinegar and combine **5 Sec. / Speed 2**. Leave to sit covered in the mixing bowl for 1 hour. If you need to do something with your Thermi in the meantime, just transfer the mixture to a bowl and cover with cling film.
2. Place half the mixture aside and crush the other half in the mixing bowl **5 Sec. / Speed 10**. Scrape down using spatula. Repeat **5 Sec. / Speed 10**. Add the other half of the mustard seeds, honey, salt, black pepper, turmeric powder, paprika and sunflower oil and combine **10 Sec. / Speed 4**.
3. Transfer into a sterilised jar (you can read about sterilising a jar in the beginning of this chapter) and keep in the fridge for up to 1 month. The mustard will become less tangy as it develops in the fridge, so I suggest you wait for a day before using it, to allow it to lose its immediate sharpness and become smooth and tasty.

roll your pesto

Pesto 'rolls' my life. I could have it on almost anything. And it is so easy to make at home and freeze so that you always have some individual portions ready. For this recipe, you can even use unpeeled garlic cloves. The pesto is sliced into individual portions and stores well in the freezer for up to three months.

makes 6
portions

200g Parmesan cheese
100g fresh basil
2 cloves garlic
100g pine nuts
100g cashews
½ tsp salt
100g olive oil
1 lemon, zest and juice

pesto rosso variation:
add 100g sundried tomatoes to the previous
  ingredients

1. Place the Parmesan, fresh basil, garlic cloves, pine nuts, cashews, salt, olive oil and lemon zest in the mixing bowl. Insert the mixing bowl lid and the measuring cup. Pour the juice onto the lid so that it drips into the mixing bowl around the measuring cup. Discard the pips that gather around the lid. Blitz **10 Sec. / Speed 10**.
2. Scrape down and blitz again **5 Sec. / Speed 7**. You can either pour the pesto straight over your pasta or into a sterilised jar (you can read about sterilising a jar at the beginning of this chapter). It keeps well in the fridge for up to 3 days.
3. If you want to freeze it, place it on a piece of greaseproof paper, carefully roll into a log and wrap like a piece of candy. Freeze. After 2 hours in the freezer, unwrap and slice into into individual portions – you should get 4–6. Then roll up again and wrap like candy. Freeze for up to 3 months.
4. To use from frozen, simply defrost the number of slices you want overnight or put straight in the pan to melt and heat up.

I will learn: — How to grate cheese using the Thermomix
                          — How to blend ingredients into a smooth paste

hidden veg tomato sauce

This tomato sauce has been around in my family for many years. I inherited the recipe from my grandma who originally got it from an Italian soldier. He used to cook it for her and added a lot of parsley to the recipe, which I find overpowering, so I changed the original slightly. It is the perfect freezer sauce to always keep a portion of at home for when you are in a hurry, and is perfect for the kids if they are fussy eaters who don't like veg. You can also fry some mince and add the sauce in later on to make a simple bolognese. It also makes a great soup base.

makes
6–8
portions

1 onion, halved
1 leek, in small chunks
2 garlic cloves
30g olive oil
2 celery sticks, in small chunks
1 carrot, in small chunks
1 courgette, in small chunks
3 chestnut mushrooms
1 red pepper, in small chunks

300g butternut squash, in small chunks
10g fresh basil
2 tsp dried oregano
2 tins plum tomatoes
30g tomato purée
1½ tsp salt
½ tsp sugar
1 tsp black pepper

1. Place the onions, leek and garlic cloves in the mixing bowl. Blitz **3 Sec. / Speed 5**.
2. Add the olive oil and fry **10 Min. / 120°C / Speed 1**.
3. Add the celery sticks, carrot, courgette, chestnut mushrooms, red pepper, butternut squash, basil leaves and dried oregano. Blitz with the help of your spatula inserted through the lid **10 Sec. / Speed 5**. Scrape down using spatula.
4. Add the plum tomatoes, tomato purée, salt, sugar and black pepper and blitz **5 Sec. / Speed 5**. Then cook **30 Min. / 100°C / Speed 2.5 / no measuring cup**. Instead of the measuring cup, place the simmering basket on top of the lid to avoid any splatters on the surface. Important: After 10 minutes, turn the speed down to 1.
5. Now you can either pour the cooked tomato sauce into sterilised jars (you can read about sterilising a jar at the beginning of this chapter) or fill freezer bags with individual portions and freeze for up to 3 months. This batch makes about 6–8 portions.

I will learn: — How to grate cheese using the Thermomix
— How to reduce a sauce

butter up, baby

This is the best basic recipe for you to always keep in mind. You can easily make your own butter at home and this recipe teaches you a great way to use your simmering basket to strain the butter from the buttermilk. Use the leftover buttermilk to make some lovely scones (p.145). With this recipe you get approx. 350g butter, perfect for making flavoured butters. You can also freeze the butter and defrost it as you need it.

basic butter recipe

makes 350g

700g double cream

1. Insert the whisk attachment.
2. Place the double cream in the mixing bowl. Whip on **Speed 4** while closely watching it until it becomes thick, beginning to churn and produce buttermilk. You can tell as soon as whisking starts becoming very loud and the butter is bashing about inside your mixing bowl. Usually it takes 1–2 minutes, so just stay with your Thermi and watch it.
3. Remove the whisk attachment and pour the butter into the simmering basket placed on top of a large bowl. Strain the butter using your spatula and really press it against the side of the bowl so that all the buttermilk is released. Make sure to keep the buttermilk and use it for baking. It can be stored in a sterilised jar (you can read about sterilising a jar at the beginning of this chapter) for up to 1 week.
4. The butter can now be placed on a piece of cling film and rolled up, wrapping it like a piece of candy. Store in the fridge or freezer.

all the flavours you need

Garlic herb:

> **2 garlic cloves**
> **5g fresh dill**
> **5g fresh chives**
> **5g fresh basil**
> **5g fresh parsley**
> **½ tsp salt**
> Blitz **3 Sec. / Speed 10**.

Sundried tomatoes:

> **5 sundried tomatoes**
> **¼ tsp salt**
> **¼ red pepper, in small chunks**
> Blitz **3 Sec. / Speed 7**.

Cranberry:

> **20g cranberries**
> **1 orange, zest**
> Blitz **4 Sec. / Speed 10**.
> Add **1 tsp maple syrup**.

Add 85g butter to the chopped ingredients and combine **10 Sec. / Speed 3**. Pour onto a piece of cling film and wrap tightly. Store in the fridge for up to 3 days or freeze for up to 1 month.

get spicy

Curry paste is a perfect freezer essential that you can always use at home on a rainy day. One curry paste 'egg' is enough for two people. Once you've made the Thai green curry paste, you can add one can of coconut milk to the leftovers in the mixing bowl to make a fabulous quick Thai soup. Add some chicken breast pieces to the simmering basket and cook for **15 Min / 100°C / Speed 1**. No waste, perfect soup and perfect spice pastes.

thai green curry paste

makes 12
portions

1 tsp cumin seeds
2 garlic cloves
2 shallots, peeled and halved
50g fresh ginger, in small pieces
5 fresh kaffir lime leaves
20g sunflower oil

20g fish sauce
4 green chillies
20g desiccated coconut
30g fresh coriander
2 sticks lemongrass, in small chunks
1 lime, juice

1. Toast the cumin seeds in a dry frying pan, then tip into the mixing bowl.
2. Add the garlic cloves, shallots, ginger, kaffir lime leaves, sunflower oil, fish sauce, green chillies, desiccated coconut, fresh coriander, lemongrass and lime juice to the mixing bowl. Blitz **5 Sec. / Speed 10**. Scrape down. Insert the simmering basket and blitz again **5 Sec. / Speed 10**.

jalfrezi curry paste

makes 12
portions

2 tsp cumin seeds
1 tsp each coriander, fenugreek, black
   mustard seeds
2 garlic cloves
50g fresh ginger, in small pieces
1 tsp ground turmeric

½ tsp sea salt flakes
20g sunflower oil
90g tomato purée
1 red chilli
15g fresh coriander, stalks cut into 3cm pieces
½ lemon, juice

1. Toast the cumin, coriander, fenugreek and black mustard seeds in a dry frying pan, then tip into the mixing bowl. Insert the simmering basket and blitz **10 Sec. / Speed 10**.
2. Remove the simmering basket and add the garlic cloves, ginger, turmeric, sea salt flakes, sunflower oil, tomato purée, red chilli, fresh coriander and lemon juice. Blitz 3–4 times **2 Sec. / Speed 10**, scraping down in between, until the mixture is smooth.
3. Line an egg box with cling film and divide the mixture between the individual holes. Freeze.

In this chapter you will learn how to make delicious food without cooking. Raw food is a great element of Thermomixing. On a hot summer's day or when you are not feeling like cooking, follow these simple recipes and enjoy with the whole family.

....

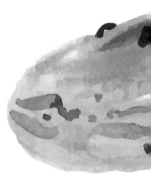

raw food

chopping guide

Veggies

	Amounts	Time/Speed
Carrots	3 carrots, in chunks	4 Sec. / Speed 5
Celery	3 sticks, in chunks	3 Sec. / Speed 5
Garlic	2 cloves, peeled	2 Sec. / Speed 5
Ginger	5cm piece, in chunks	4 Sec. / Speed 7
Onions	1 onion, peeled & halved	2 Sec. / Speed 5
Potatoes	3 potatoes, quartered	3 Sec. / Speed 4
Red cabbage / White cabbage	½ cabbage, in chunks	10 Sec. / Speed 4

Fruit

	Amounts	Time/Speed
Apples	600g, cut into pieces	4–5 Sec. / Speed 4
Pears	600g, cut into pieces	3–4 Sec. / Speed 4

Herbs

	Amounts	Time/Speed
Basil	20g	3 Sec. / Speed 8
Dill		
Coriander		
Mint		
Parsley		

Meat

	Amounts	Time/Speed
Beef chuck	300g cut into pieces (3 cm)	10 Sec. / Speed 6
Chicken breast		
Pork shoulder		
Turkey breast		

Milling

	Amounts	Time/Speed
Cheese (medium)	200g, cut into pieces	10 Sec. / Speed 5
Cheese (hard)	100g, cut into pieces	15 Sec. / Speed 10
Peppercorns, coarse	10g	30 Sec. / Speed 10
Rice	100g	1 Min. / Speed 10
Whole spices	20g	1 Min. / Speed 9

Emulsifying

	Amounts	Time/Speed
Salad dressing	200g	20 Sec. / Speed 3

the simmering basket

'The unexpected multitasker'

The simmering basket is a truly amazing element of the Thermomix. It is a real multitasker and can help you become so efficient with a few extra tricks. It is inserted in the mixing bowl and usually used to cook rice, potatoes, eggs, pork loin or small chunks of fish. But it can do so much more than that.

did you know?

You can boil or poach eggs using the simmering basket. Depending on how soft you want your eggs, you can leave them in for as long as 15 minutes. Use the simmering basket when making jam; to get a really smooth preserve, simply pass the cooked jam through the simmering basket and use the spatula to press it through, discarding any leftovers.

If you want to reduce a sauce, remove the measuring cup and place the simmering basket on top of the mixing bowl instead. It will help let the steam through and reduce sauces to achieve a thicker consistency. For smaller quantities of spices, insert the simmering basket into the mixing bowl before grinding to prevent them from flying up the sides of the bowl away from the blade.

After you have made fresh lemonade or orange juice, use the simmering basket to strain any bits of fruit, leaving a smooth juice in your jug. and only keep the smooth juice in your jug. Use the simmering basket to strain your pasta – no more colanders needed.

The simmering basket is also great for straining cooked legumes. Anything thick enough not to fall through the slits can be strained using the simmering basket. My absolute favourite thing to make with the simmering basket is potatoes and pork fillet. Simply cut the pork into thick slices of about 3–4cm and place in the bottom of the simmering basket. Add a few potatoes and fill up the mixing bowl with water. Cook for 20–30 minutes depending on the softness of the potatoes. The simmering basket ensures you cook the meat gently and it gets really juicy, almost like poached meat.

Whole beetroot and sweet potatoes are very happy in the simmering basket, too. Because the water comes into contact with most of those ingredients, they will cook faster, leaving you with perfectly al dente veggies.

my food prep routine

Food prep is the cool way of saying: I am going to spend a lot of time in the kitchen chopping up veggies and cooking food that I will need for next week. But it does work and makes a big difference to your eating routine. I have a food preparation routine at home and always make sure certain things are ready for cooking. Smaller ingredients like onions are always in the freezer, pre-chopped, so that I can immediately use them for frying. Sunday night is my food prep night and I make sure that I prepare as much as I possibly can. I have observed that if I do not have certain food prepared then I tend to snack more, which always results in my feeling lethargic, not being able to concentrate and having naughty things at home, like those super lovely but devilish chocolate bars.

Some of the things that I prepare at home include my favourite salad dressings so that I can whizz up a salad in no time at lunch or as a side dish for dinner. I store them in mason jars in the fridge and they last all week.

Because we love spaghetti bolognese (p.112) at home, I usually prepare the veggies I need, such as carrots, celery sticks, onions and garlic in one go and freeze them uncooked in batches. I can then just take the individual portions out the night before and leave them to thaw. It makes it so much easier when you are under time pressure.

Beetroot burgers are also a must for me at home and I always have some in the freezer for a quick lunch or dinner. Even if you are short of time, the best thing you can do is chop your veggies in the Thermi, boil eggs, cook potatoes, beetroot and sweet potatoes, prepare a few dips and salad dressings and maybe one loaf of bread. That is already enough to get you through most of the week in terms of breakfasts, lunches and snacks. On top of that, I usually have a few snacks ready, such as ice lollies (p.73) or raw beetroot balls (p.66), which give you a great energy kick when you are feeling tired.

For food preparation, a little goes a long way. Even if you spend a little extra time in the evening chopping up and freezing a few portions of veggies bought that day, you have already done more than most people would. If you can, on top of that, buy veggies and fruit that are in season. They taste much better and they are easier to source.

top secret tips

1   If you are unsure of how big veggie chunks should be before putting them in the mixing bowl, test whether they fit through the lid opening first. If they fit, they are small enough to be handled by the blade. When checking carrots, pass the pieces through the lid opening widthways.

2   To chop fresh herbs without bruising them, chop them on turbo 3–4 times for 1 second. It will keep them fresh without releasing any bitter aromas.

3   To grind spices, dry fry your whole spices first in a large non-stick frying pan without oil, then tip into the mixing bowl. Place the simmering basket on top and grind **10 Sec. / Speed 10**. The simmering basket will prevent the spices from going everywhere.

4   If you want to grate cheese that is a little softer than Parmesan, place 1 tsp plain flour for 100g cheese in the mixing bowl. **Grate 7 Sec. / Speed 9**.

5   To peel garlic, place between 2 and 10 cloves in the mixing bowl. Blitz **5 Sec. / Reverse / Speed 5**. The cloves will be chopped but the skins will remain large. Add 200g water to the mixing bowl and wait until the skins float to the top. Remove with a scoop and drain the water through the simmering basket. You will be left with gorgeous chopped garlic.

6   To make mayonnaise more easily, add the oil through the mixing bowl lid with the measuring cup in place. The measuring cup will prevent the oil from pouring down too fast and make a smoother mayonnaise.

7   The reverse mode is perfect for combining ingredients without chopping them at all. It is ideal if you are combining a salad with a dressing or when you want to preserve some chunky bits in a dip. Simply press the reverse button before setting the speed.

8   Smoothies get their best consistency when you blend them for **1 Min. / Speed 10**. During this time, the cells of the fruit are split up to achieve the desired smoothness.

overnight oats

Overnight oats are a modern twist on the classic porridge. I absolutely love preparing oats for breakfast. They are so versatile, you can pretty much create any flavouring you like and they keep so well in the fridge, and also fill you up from breakfast to lunch. The perfect breakfast companion. You can use homemade almond milk from p.38 to make the oats.

raspberry

makes 2
portions

200g raspberries
40g honey
½ lemon, juice
20g chia seeds

200g gluten free oats
500g almond milk
1 tsp vanilla extract

1. Place the raspberries, 10g honey, lemon juice and 10g chia seeds in the mixing bowl. **Blitz 5 Sec. / Speed 6**.
2. Pour into a small bowl until later. Rinse the mixing bowl.
3. Place the oats, almond milk, vanilla extract, remaining 30g honey and remaining 10g chia seeds in the mixing bowl. Combine **10 Sec. / Speed 2.5**.
4. Layer the oats and raspberries in a large mason jar and refrigerate overnight.

chocolate

makes 2
portions

1 banana
200g gluten free oats
500g almond milk

20g cocoa powder
20g honey
20g flaked almonds

1. Place the banana in the mixing bowl. Blitz **10 Sec. / Speed 4**. Scrape down.
2. Add the oats, almond milk, cocoa powder, honey and flaked almonds and combine **10 Sec. / Speed 2.5**.
3. Pour the oats into a large mason jar and refrigerate overnight.

You can take the oats to work with you the next morning and have them cold or warm them up in the microwave for 1 minute. The mixture is enough for 2 portions and will keep in the fridge for up to 3 days.

I will learn: — How to create a fast breakfast without hassle that is durable
— How to use the mix function to combine ingredients without blending

raw beet balls

Energy balls are a superb way of filling you up between meals. This is one of the most amazing things I have tried and is so colourful you will definitely remember it. These super tasty raw beet balls are almost a sweet treat and you can freeze them easily in individual portions. Thaw as needed. They keep well in the fridge for up to a week.

makes
12 balls

100g desiccated coconut + extra for rolling
100g cashew nuts
1 raw beetroot, peeled and chopped into
  large chunks

6 medjool dates, pitted
½ tsp vanilla extract

1. Place the desiccated coconut, cashew nuts, beetroot, medjool dates and vanilla extract in the mixing bowl. Blitz **10 Sec / Speed 10**.
2. Form into small balls using wet hands and roll in extra desiccated coconut. Refrigerate. You can also freeze them and thaw as needed.

Top secret tip: If you don't fancy raw beetroot, you can replace it with more cashew nuts and make delicious coconut cashew balls.

key lime smoothie

Key lime pie is one of the best desserts in the history of dessert making. Imagine starting your day with a smoothie that tastes just like the pie but is totally vegan and drinkable? Try this super delicious Key lime smoothie and transform your breakfast on the go routine.

makes
2 glasses

450g almond milk (p.38)
1 banana
30g fresh spinach
2 limes, juice and zest

½ tsp vanilla extract
3 digestive biscuits
2 medjool dates, pitted

1. Place the almond milk, banana, spinach, lime juice and zest, vanilla extract, digestive biscuits and medjool dates in the mixing bowl. Blitz **1 Min. / Speed 10**. Pour into glasses and take with you to work or have it as breakfast on the go.

I will learn: How to make a perfectly smooth drink out of whole fruit using the blending function

fro-yo bites

If you are looking for a quick treat for the kids, these frozen yoghurt bites are absolutely brilliant. Packed with super delicious ingredients such as bananas and peanuts, I nearly ate all of the yoghurt before freezing it. They keep well in the freezer for up to three months and you can also dip them into melted chocolate once frozen. Almost like a healthy Magnum.

makes
48 bites

3 bananas
100g peanut butter
250g greek style yoghurt
20g agave nectar

1. Place the bananas, peanut butter, greek style yoghurt and agave nectar in the mixing bowl. Blitz 10 Sec. / Speed 6.
2. Pour into small silicone moulds or popsicle moulds and freeze for at least 4 hours.

Top secret tip: Place 200g dark chocolate, in small pieces, in the mixing bowl. Chop **7 Sec.** / **Speed 9**. Scrape down, then melt **3 Min.** / **37°C** / **Speed 2**. Dip each frozen yoghurt bite into the chocolate and place on a piece of greaseproof paper for 5 minutes to harden. Then return to the freezer or eat immediately.

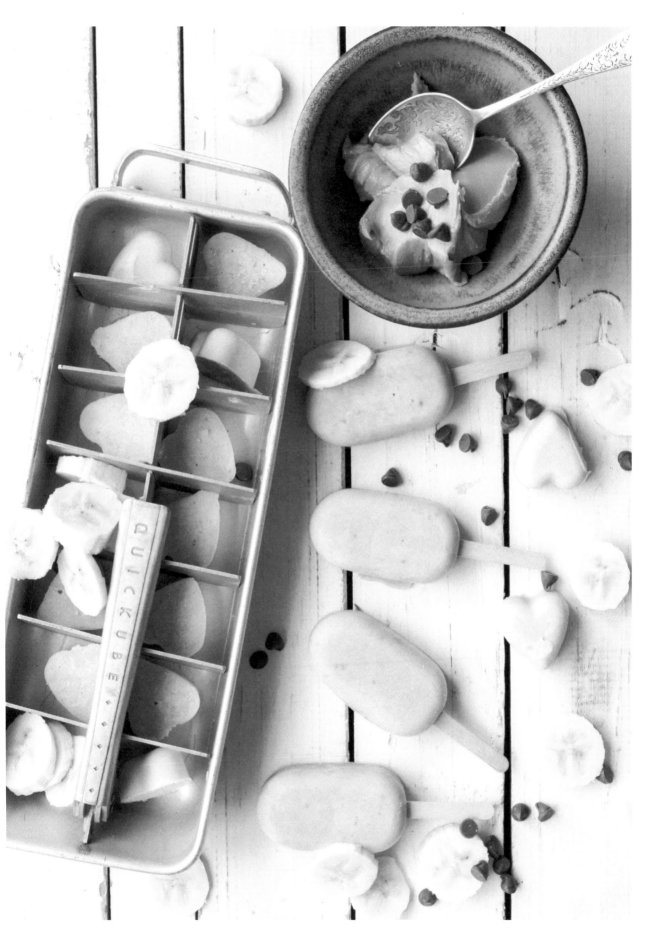

popsicle love

Who doesn't love a bit of popsicle in their life? These super delicious popsicles are the perfect addition to your freezer. The matcha ice cream almost tastes like pistachios without containing any nuts and both recipes are perfectly suitable for children. You can add some vodka to the mixture if you want to make an adult-only dessert and have an even smoother texture.

strawberry peach

makes 6 popsicles

2 peaches, stones removed
300g strawberries

75g agave nectar
1 can full fat coconut milk

1. Place the peaches, strawberries and 25g agave nectar in the mixing bowl. Blitz **5 Sec. / Speed 7**. Pour into a jug and set aside until later.
2. Rinse the bowl. Add the coconut milk and remaining 50g agave nectar and combine **10 Sec. / Speed 2.5**.
3. Pour the coconut milk and puréed fruit, alternating between the two, into popsicle forms and freeze for at least 8 hours.
4. You can add 1 Tbsp vodka to the coconut milk to avoid freezing and create a smoother texture, but make sure not to serve that to kids.

matcha

makes 6 popsicles

1 ripe avocado, stone removed
½ lemon, juice
30g agave nectar
30g coconut oil

½ tsp vanilla extract
40g peanut butter
170g coconut milk
½ tsp matcha powder

1. Place the avocado, lemon juice, agave nectar, coconut oil, vanilla extract, peanut butter, coconut milk and matcha powder in the mixing bowl. Combine **10 Sec. / Speed 7**.
2. Pour the mixture into popsicle forms and freeze for at least 8 hours.

cherry bakewell ice cream

Cherry Bakewell tart is one of my all time favourites. Since I came to the UK, I have come across many lovely tarts and cakes that I had never seen before, so I decided to develop a little twist on the classic in the form of ice cream. Warning: this is an adult ice cream and contains vodka. The vodka prevents the ice cream from freezing too much and gives it a smoother texture. If you have children, simply leave the vodka out and give the ice cream a bit more time to defrost before serving.

serves
4–6

1 can coconut milk
1 Tbsp cornflour
60g agave nectar
200g pitted cherries

1 tsp almond extract
5g vodka
¼ tsp xanthan gum
½ tsp beetroot powder

1. Place coconut milk, cornflour, agave nectar, cherries, almond extract, vodka, xanthan gum and beetroot powder in the mixing bowl. Combine **30 Sec. / Speed 6**.
2. Pour into a large container and freeze for at least 8 hours. Remove from the freezer 15 minutes before using.

raw detox salad

There is nothing better than a feel-good salad for lunch. This one has all the veggies you need. Don't waste the broccoli stem; it is just as tasty and produces a great crunch in the salad. You can easily freeze the chopped broccoli, cabbage and herbs in individual freezer bags and defrost for a great work lunch. A foodie approach to a classic Thermomix salad.

serves
4

1 broccoli, florets picked and stem
   chopped in large chunks
200g red cabbage, in small chunks
10g fresh coriander, stalks chopped
   in 3cm pieces
10g fresh parsley
40g kale

25g coconut shavings
10g mixed seeds
1 can chickpeas, drained
1 serving lemon tahini dressing (p.79)
1 grapefruit, peeled and sliced
1 avocado, sliced

1. Place the broccoli, red cabbage, coriander, parsley and kale in the mixing bowl. Blitz **3 Sec. / Speed 5**. If you want it finer, blitz it a bit more.
2. Add the coconut shavings, mixed seeds, chickpeas and lemon tahini dressing and combine **40 Sec. / Reverse / Speed 2.5**.
3. Tip into a large salad bowl. Decorate with slices of grapefruit and avocado.

I will learn: How to use the chopping function to chop veg into edible chunks

best salad dressings

I am always on the lookout for the perfect salad dressing. I've compiled my favourite dressings that you can use for any salad you want. The lemon tahini dressing goes particularly well with the raw detox salad on p.76. If you are taking a salad to work for lunch, wrap the sauce in a bit of cling film and put it on top of the salad so that both stay fresh. Alternatively, you can store it in a jar in the fridge for up to one week. **Each is enough for 1 large salad.**

orange vinaigrette

1 orange, juice
20g honey
40g cider vinegar
10g olive oil
½ tsp sea salt flakes
½ tsp black pepper

1. Place the orange juice, honey, cider vinegar, olive oil, sea salt flakes and black pepper in the mixing bowl. Emulsify 20 Sec. / Speed 4.

honey mustard dressing

30g wholegrain mustard
30g honey
50g cider vinegar
20g olive oil
½ tsp sea salt flakes
½ tsp black pepper

1. Place wholegrain mustard, honey, cider vinegar, olive oil, sea salt flakes and black pepper in the mixing bowl. Emulsify 20 Sec. / Speed 4.

yoghurt dressing

100g greek style yoghurt
5g dried oregano
20g white wine vinegar
½ tsp sea salt flakes
½ tsp black pepper
10g olive oil

1. Place the greek style yoghurt, dried oregano, white wine vinegar, sea salt flakes, black pepper, and olive oil in the mixing bowl. Emulsify 20 Sec. / Speed 4.

lemon tahini dressing

50g tahini
20g olive oil
½ tsp soy sauce
2 lemons, zest of 1 and juice of 2
½ tsp sea salt flakes
½ tsp black pepper

1. Place the tahini, olive oil, soy sauce, lemon zest and juice, sea salt flakes and black pepper in the mixing bowl. Emulsify 20 Sec. / Speed 2.5.

cacik dip

My partner Jesse is completely obsessed with Mediterranean food. This is actually one of his favourite dips to make and it has always been our go-to recipe for a quick party snack. You can serve it with homemade pitta chips (p.136) and it is best eaten fresh with a nice glass of wine.

serves
4

2 garlic cloves, peeled
2–3 sprigs fresh mint, twigs removed
2–3 sprigs fresh dill
1 cucumber, halved and flesh removed
  with a spoon

400g Greek style yoghurt
1 tsp sea salt
½ tsp black pepper
¼ tsp chilli powder
¼ tsp ground cumin

1. Place the garlic cloves, mint and dill in the mixing bowl. Blitz **4 Sec. / Speed 7**. Scrape down using spatula.
2. Add the cucumber and chop **4 Sec. / Speed 5**.
3. Add the yoghurt, sea salt, black pepper, chilli powder and ground cumin. Combine **10 Sec. / Reverse / Speed 3**.
4. Keep refrigerated and serve with Parmesan rosemary shortbread (p.142) or pitta chips (p.136).

I will learn: — How to chop garlic finely
                  — How to use the reverse speed function

black forest mousse

We all know the classic Black Forest gâteau. What a retro cake. All that cream and chocolate makes it a calorie bomb for sure. This amazing twist on the classic dessert is so light and fluffy and contains no refined sugar; it's totally amazing. If you want to serve it to children, simply use cherry juice instead of the kirsch, which is a traditional brandy found in Germany.

makes
4

200g sour cherries (or fresh, pitted
   and halved)
10g kirsch (or brandy)

1 ripe avocado, pitted
6 dates, pitted
20g agave nectar
200g coconut milk
40g cocoa powder
1 tsp vanilla extract

50g coconut cream (or the creamy top
   of a can of coconut milk)
20g cacao nibs

1. Soak the cherries in the kirsch or brandy in a small bowl and place aside.
2. Place the avocado, dates, agave nectar, coconut milk, cocoa powder and vanilla extract in the mixing bowl. Blitz **30 Sec. / Speed 7**. Scrape down with spatula. Blitz again **10 Sec. / Speed 7**.
3. Pour the mixture into small dessert bowls. Top with some coconut cream, cacao nibs and cherries. Refrigerate for at least 2 hours before serving.

I will learn: If you want to freeze the Black Forest mousse, simply do that before you add the cherries or coconut cream. Thaw as needed and decorate when it is ready.

In this chapter you will get your hands on some of the most amazing cooking tricks for the Thermomix. From all-in-one meals to learning how to use your Varoma, be prepared for some yummy food.

....

cooking

cooking guide

Hard Veggies

Add 800g water or broth to the mixing bowl. Place the ingredients into the Varoma dish and tray then steam. The following guides are based on a portion for four, i.e. four handfuls. If the lower tray gets full, place the remaining ingredients in the upper tray where possible.

	Size	*Setting*
Aubergine	2cm cubes	25 Min. / Varoma / Speed 1
Beetroot		40 Min. / Varoma / Speed 1
Butternut squash		30 Min. / Varoma / Speed 1
Carrots	1cm slices	25 Min. / Varoma / Speed 1
Celeriac	2cm cubes	

Soft Veggies

	Size	*Setting*
Asparagus	whole stems	20 Min. / Varoma / Speed 1
Beans, green	whole	15 Min. / Varoma / Speed 1
Broccoli	small florets	20 Min. / Varoma / Speed 1
Cauliflower		
Celery	2cm cubes	20 Min. / Varoma / Speed 1
Courgette	2cm slices	20 Min. / Varoma / Speed 1
Fennel		25 Min. / Varoma / Speed 1
Leeks		20 Min. / Varoma / Speed 1
Mushrooms	whole	20 Min. / Varoma / Speed 1
Radishes	2cm cubes	
Peas (frozen)	whole	15 Min. / Varoma / Speed 1
Peppers (red, yellow)	2cm slices	
Spinach	whole leaves	10 Min. / Varoma / Speed 1

Beans & Grains

Add 600g water or broth to the mixing bowl. Place the ingredients into the simmering basket and cook.

	Amount	*Setting*
Black beans	250g, pre-soaked for minimum 8 hrs	1 Hour / Varoma / Speed 1
Chickpeas		1 Hour / Varoma / Speed 1
Kidney beans		45 Min. / Varoma / Speed 1
Lentils	250g	40 Min. / Varoma / Speed 1
Millet		20 Min. / Varoma / Speed 1
Potatoes	500g, quartered	30 Min. / Varoma / Speed 1
Potatoes, sweet		
Quinoa	250g	25 Min. / Varoma / Speed 1

Rice

Add 1100g water or broth to the mixing bowl. Place the ingredients into the simmering basket and cook at the stated temperature. After half the cooking time, reduce the temperature to 100°C.

	Amount	*Setting*
Rice, brown	250g	1 Hour / Varoma / Speed 1
Rice, white		30 Min. / Varoma / Speed 1
Rice, wild		50 Min. / Varoma / Speed 1

Fish / Seafood

Add 800g water to the mixing bowl. Place the ingredients into the Varoma dish and steam. If there is not enough room in the dish, place the remaining ingredients on the Varoma tray.

	Amount	*Setting*
Cod	2 fillets, whole	20 Min. / Varoma / Speed 1
Haddock		
Mussels	25 mussels, whole	
Prawns	20 prawns, whole	
Salmon	2 fillets, whole	
Trout		

Meat

Add 800g water to the mixing bowl. Place the ingredients into the Varoma dish and steam. If there is not enough room in the dish, place the remaining ingredients on the Varoma tray.

	Amount	*Setting*
Beef roasting joint	1kg, whole	50 Min. / Varoma / Speed 1
Chicken, whole		45 Min. / Varoma / Speed 1
Chicken breast	4 breasts, whole	25 Min. / Varoma / Speed 1
Frankfurters	6 sausages, whole	15 Min. / Varoma / Speed 1
Meatballs	4cm in diameter	25 Min. / Varoma / Speed 1

Puréeing

For mashed potatoes/sweet potatoes, add 20g butter, 150g milk, 1 pinch nutmeg and ½ tsp salt to the mixing bowl before whisking.

	Amount	*Setting*
Broad bean mash	500g, whole, cooked	15 sec. / Speed 3 / Butterfly whisk
Fruit mash (pears or apples)	500g, 2cm pieces, cooked	30 sec. / Speed 3 / Butterfly whisk
Mushy peas	500g, whole, cooked	15 sec. / Speed 3 / Butterfly whisk
Potato mash	500g, 2.5cm cubes, cooked	30 sec. / Speed 3 / Butterfly whisk
Sweet potato mash		

Fruit

Add 800g water to the mixing bowl. Place the ingredients into the Varoma dish and steam. If there is not enough room in the dish, place the remaining ingredients on the Varoma tray.

	Amount	*Setting*
Apples	500g, quartered	15 Min. / Varoma / Speed 1
Apricots	500g, halved, pitted	
Cherries		
Peaches	500g, halved	
Pears	800g, quartered	20 Min. / Varoma / Speed 1
Strawberries	500g, halved	15 Min. / Varoma / Speed 1

the varoma

'Let the steam out'

The Varoma is one of the most revolutionary ways of cooking your food in a healthy and gentle way. It is also known as the steaming attachment and comes in three parts: the Varoma dish and lid, which you always use, and the optional Varoma tray. You can steam any food, including veggies, fruit, meat and fish, and you can even sterilise jars in the Varoma. There are some basics tricks to using the Varoma and if you haven't explored it yet, it is time to get it out of the cupboard and place it right on top of the kitchen counter.

did you know?

When you are steaming any food in the Varoma make sure to leave some space for the steam to circulate. A few holes need to stay uncovered. Fish and veggies, except for potatoes, are perfect for the Varoma because they cook quickly. If you want to prevent the juices from escaping through the holes, take a piece of greaseproof paper or a ready cut Varoma liner (see my online shop), wet it and line the Varoma tray with it. Then place your fish on top.

The Varoma dish, which is the larger part of your Varoma, is usually used for larger ingredients, such as chicken or larger amounts of veggies, whereas the Varoma tray is better for fish and veggies that cook faster. Occasionally I even use my Varoma to steam cakes. Instead of baking your cheesecake, make a smaller quantity, wrap the bottom in aluminium foil and pour 1000g water into the mixing bowl. The cheesecake dish needs to fit the Varoma dish and it is best to add a few aluminium foil balls to the bottom before placing the cheesecake on top so that the steam can circulate. Cover the cake tightly with cling film and steam for **1–1.5 Hrs. / Varoma / Speed 1**. In between, top up the water if needed.

my cooking routine

Cooking to me is the most relaxing and almost therapeutic activity of the day. I like to unwind and listen to my favourite music while preparing dinner for Jesse and me. We cook together with our Thermi and even on a busy day we always find time to cook food from scratch. One of my go-to elements of the Thermomix is the Varoma. I use it for a lot of different things, for example steaming a whole chicken. My favourite recipe is Hainanese chicken rice, and preparing a whole chicken in the Varoma really adds some additional flavour and juiciness to the cooked chicken.

I place the whole chicken in the Varoma dish and add 2 vegetable stock cubes to the water in the mixing bowl. I tend to makes small cuts in the skin so that the juices can really soak through. Also, a little trick is to score the leg and wing bones with a knife so that it breaks open the marrow, which helps release juices. Then I steam the chicken for about **45–60 Min. / Varoma / Speed 1** until cooked through and it reaches target temperature (see guide on pp.88–91). After 30 minutes, I insert the simmering basket filled with basmati rice into the mixing bowl and cook that simultaneously. It is one of the juiciest chickens you will ever have. Served with some chilli dipping sauce, it makes my day. I use the leftover stock as chicken/veggie stock and preserve it in a jar to cook a gorgeous soup the next day.

We are both big fans of Indian cuisine, so most of the recipes I cook with the Thermi are coconut dal (p.104) or chicken curries. Some other recipes that you can find in this chapter which are super tasty are cauliflower soup with roasted chick-peas (p.106) and also a super delicious roast beef with celeriac mash (p.114). This dish is also prepared in the Varoma and, my gosh, it is such a succulent piece of meat. If you haven't tried sous vide cooking before and have no idea what I am talking about right now, don't worry. The technique for making the juiciest roast beef can be found on p.114 without having to learn all about sous vide.

Another thing I really like to do is spice up rice. Whether I add some vegetable stock paste to the water in the mixing bowl, flavour the rice with some cinnamon sticks or add in some black beans, there are so many possibilities to make it a unique element of your dish.

Here are two of my favourite versions for flavoured rice. You can find another one of my specialities, rice & peas on p.110 as part of my jerk chicken recipe. You will notice that I only cook with basmati rice. My favourite brand is Tilda, and I have been experimenting with rice a lot. This has to be my favourite rice because it turns out so fluffy. I use a special technique by which I steam the rice for the first half, then stir with a fork and turn down the temperature to finish it off. It does prevent the rice from being too soggy.

Yellow Rice (aka Nasi Kuning)

This rice is the perfect side dish for South-East Asian dishes. Place 250g basmati rice in the simmering basket. Add 4 kaffir lime leaves, 2 lemongrass stalks (halved) and 25g peeled ginger, in long strips, to the simmering basket. Add 650g water, 1 can coconut milk and 1 tsp ground turmeric powder to the mixing bowl. Cook **15 Min. / Varoma / Speed 1**. Stir the rice with a fork, then cook again **15 Min. / 100°C / Speed 1**.

Pilau Rice

This is the ideal rice to serve with Indian food. I love it as a side dish for coconut dal (p.104). First, place 1 onion (halved) into the mixing bowl. Chop **2 Sec. / Speed 5**. Then add 30g ghee and 1 star anise and fry **10 Min. / 120°C / Speed 1**. Transfer into a bowl. Add 1050g water to the mixing bowl (no need to clean in between). Place 250g basmati rice in the simmering basket. Add the fried onions, 10g flaked almonds, 10g raisins, 1 cinnamon stick, 3 cardamom pods, 1 clove and 1 star anise. Cook **15 Min. / Varoma / Speed 1**. Stir the rice with a fork, then cook again **15 Min. / 100°C / Speed 1**. Remove the cinnamon stick, cardamom pods, clove and star anise and serve.

top secret tips

1 To spice up your rice, add 1 can coconut milk and 700g water to the mixing bowl. Insert 250g basmati rice and cook **30 Min. / Varoma / Speed 0.5**. After 15 minutes, turn down the heat to 100°C and give it a quick stir through the lid with the spatula.

2 You can easily make shredded chicken by simply steaming a couple of whole chicken breasts in the Varoma for 25 minutes. Drain the water and place the chicken breasts, chopped in half, in the mixing bowl. Chop **4–7 Sec. / Reverse / Speed 4** until desired size is achieved. You can also freeze the finished chicken in individual portions.

3 After making stock paste and dividing it into portions, don't waste the residue in the mixing bowl. Make a soup by filling the uncleaned mixing bowl with water up to the 1l mark and cook for **15 Min. / 100°C / Speed 1**. If the weather is too hot for soup, use the recipe above to make liquid stock. Pour in jars and keep in the fridge for up to 1 month or freeze in ice cube trays.

4 After a lovely barbecue, you can easily reheat your meal in the Varoma tray **15 Min. / 80°C / Speed 1**. You can do this with any meat you have left from your barbecue, or I also do this with prawns.

5 To avoid long heating times, add the water to the mixing bowl and start heating for **5 Min. / Varoma / Speed 1** while preparing your veggies. Place the Varoma into position when the water is hot. This will give you a better indication of cooking times and you will save a few minutes that you can spend on the sofa instead.

6 To make your soups more interesting, season a few pieces of the vegetables for the soup with pepper and salt and put in the Varoma. While you are cooking your soup, the veggies will steam and add a bit of crunch to the soup at the end. Serve decorated on top of the soup. You can also roast those pieces of veggies in the oven if you want some smoky flavours.

7   My top secret piece of equipment in the kitchen when cooking meat is a Thermopen. This can be purchased from Amazon and is the most accurate way of telling when meat is cooked. I have learned not to cook any meat by time but to look at the temperature; it makes a big difference to the way your meat tastes. The Thermopen is inserted into the middle of your piece of meat and when it shows the correct temperature, your meat is done. Here are a few guidelines for you to know when meat is done:

Beef
Medium rare: **63°C**
Medium: **71°C**
Well done: **77°C**

Pork pieces and whole cuts: **71°C**
Chicken pieces (e.g. breast): **75°C**
Whole chicken: **82°C**
Fish: **70°C**
Prawns: **75°C**

8   To avoid anything sticking to the Varoma, use either a piece of greaseproof paper and wet it to line both trays or use prepared Varoma liners and follow the instructions on the packaging. You will be able to purchase these on my shop. Alternatively, grease the Varoma with butter.

9   To reduce liquids in sauces, simply take off the measuring cup and replace with the simmering basket on top of the mixing bowl lid. The simmering basket lets through some additional steam and ensures the sauce does not retain too much water.

10   The best eggs are boiled in your simmering basket. To avoid having to keep an eye on your clock, follow these timings for the perfect consistency eggs:

Very runny egg (egg yolk liquid, egg white syrupy): **10 minutes / Varoma / Speed 1**
Runny (egg yolk liquid, egg white firm : **11 minutes / Varoma / Speed 1**
Soft egg (egg yolk soft): **12 minutes / Varoma / Speed 1**
Firmly boiled egg: **13 minutes / Varoma / Speed 1**
Hard boiled egg: **15 minutes / Varoma / Speed 1**

smashed avocado eggs on toast

I really like a boiled egg for breakfast. At home, we always used to make boiled eggs for breakfast and we had to put about four different timers on because my dad wanted his super soft, then my grandma wanted hers slightly harder, then my brother and then me. I was the one who had the egg that was so hard you could have mistaken it for a rock. With your Thermi it is much easier. Serve the egg with smashed avocados and have a great breakfast.

makes 2
portions

2 eggs
500g water
1 avocado
2 slices white bloomer loaf, toasted (p.130)
10g salad cress

1 pinch sea salt flakes
1 pinch black pepper
½ lemon, juice

1. To boil the eggs, place them in the simmering basket. Fill the mixing bowl with the water and boil for **10–15 Min. / 100°C / Speed 1** (see guide on p.97).
2. Place the avocado in the mixing bowl. Blitz **10 Sec. / Speed 4**. Spread over the toast, garnish with the egg halves, cress, sea salt and black pepper and spritz with fresh lemon juice.

I will learn: How to easily boil eggs in the simmering basket

squash hummus

I am a big dip fan and this is certainly one of the creamiest versions of hummus that you can make. The roasted squash is perfect for blending with chickpeas and keeps well in the fridge for up to three days. You can use the pitta chips on p.136 or roasted carrots for dipping.

serves
4

½ butternut squash, chopped into
　small cubes
3 garlic cloves
10g olive oil
½ tsp sea salt
½ tsp black pepper
1 lemon, juice and zest
1 can chickpeas, drained

60g tahini
60g olive oil
20g fresh parsley, stalks removed
½ tsp ground cumin
¼ tsp ground smoked paprika
Pitta bread chips (p.136) and roasted carrots
　to serve

1. Preheat the oven to 200°C / 180°C Fan / Gas Mark 6. Place the butternut squash and garlic cloves onto a large rectangular baking tray lined with greaseproof paper. Toss with olive oil, salt and pepper and bake for 25–30 minutes until golden brown. Leave to cool.
2. Tip the roasted squash into the mixing bowl. Add the lemon juice and zest, chickpeas, tahini, olive oil, parsley, cumin and smoked paprika. Blitz **10 Sec. / Speed 10**. Scrape down with spatula and combine **5 Sec. / Speed 6**.
3. Serve with roasted carrots and pitta bread chips. You can freeze the squash hummus for up to 2 weeks.

Top secret tip: To make roasted carrots for dipping, place whole carrots on a baking tray lined with greaseproof paper and drizzle with olive oil. Sprinkle with salt and pepper and roast in the oven at 220°C for 20 minutes.

beetroot burgers

Now these are some colourful and vibrant burgers. They make a perfect dinner for the whole family, and if you don't fancy meat or you are vegetarian, this is an ideal and nutritious dish to go for. Serve with some fresh bread and salad and you have yourself a lovely meal. They can also be frozen before being baked in individual portions. Just make sure to cover them with a bit more polenta. You can break them up and eat on a salad cold the next day. Makes 6 burgers. Freezable.

makes 6
burgers

2 spring onions, in 4cm pieces
2 garlic cloves
½ tsp ground coriander
1 can beluga lentils, drained and rinsed
250g raw peeled beetroot in large chunks

1 pinch sea salt
1 pinch black pepper
½ lemon, zest and juice
80g polenta + extra for coating
15g fresh parsley

1. Preheat the oven to 180°C / 160°C Fan / Gas Mark 4.
2. Add the spring onions, garlic cloves, ground coriander, beluga lentils, beetroot, sea salt, black pepper, lemon zest and juice, polenta and fresh parsley to the mixing bowl. Blitz **15 Sec. / Speed 10**.
3. Prepare a large baking tray with greaseproof paper.
4. Take a small handful of the beetroot mixture and form into a burger shape. The mixture will be very sloppy so don't handle it too much; it will firm up as it bakes.
5. Once on the tray, sprinkle the tops of the burgers with some additional polenta to create a light coating and softly pat it in.
6. Bake for 15–20 minutes until crispy on the outside.

I will learn: How to use the blending function to combine ingredients smoothly, creating a compact burger mixture

coconut dal

One of my favourite cuisines is Indian. I think not a day goes past in which I don't make something Indian spiced, whether it be for breakfast, lunch or dinner. The spices and the whole process of cooking are just so much more fragrant and complex, and the flavours never get boring. This coconut dal is a perfect side dish and ideal for dipping your naan, chapatis or roti into. You can also have it as a main served with some fresh yoghurt and kachumber salad.

serves
4

300g whole red lentils
700g water
½ tsp turmeric powder
1 green chilli, sliced
200g coconut milk
4 shallots, peeled and halved
4 garlic cloves, peeled
2 dried red chillies

30g ghee (p.44)
12 curry leaves
1 star anise
1 tsp black mustard seeds
1 tsp cumin seeds
1 cinnamon stick
1 tsp ground coriander
8 plum tomatoes, each chopped into 8 pieces

1. Place the red lentils, water, turmeric powder and green chilli in the mixing bowl. Cook **30 Min. / 100°C / Reverse / Speed 0.5**.
2. Add the coconut milk and cook again **15 Min. / 100°C / Reverse / Speed 0.5**.
3. Once cooked, pour the lentils into a separate bowl and leave covered until later.
4. In the clean mixing bowl, place the shallots, garlic cloves and dried chillies. Chop **3 Sec. / Speed 5**. Scrape down with spatula. Add the ghee, curry leaves, star anise, black mustard seeds, cumin seeds, cinnamon stick and ground coriander and fry **5 Min. / 120°C / Reverse / Speed 1**.
5. Add the tomatoes and cook again **5 min. / 100°C / Reverse / Speed 1**.
6. Pour the lentils back into the mixing bowl to warm through, then serve.

Top secret tip: This dal is perfect for freezing in batches. You can cook it in advance and freeze in individual portions. Thaw and reheat by tipping into the mixing bowl and cooking it **10 Min. / 100°C / Reverse / Speed 1**.

cauliflower soup

This is one of the tastiest soups I have ever had. The roasted cauliflower and chickpeas add an incredibly smoky flavour to the soup and round it off so well. It is the perfect warming soup for a rainy day. You can easily freeze the soup in batches afterwards.

serves
4

1 cauliflower, broken into small florets
1 can chickpeas, drained and rinsed
5 garlic cloves (whole, no peeling necessary)
30g olive oil
½ tsp ground cumin
½ tsp paprika
½ tsp sea salt flakes
1 pinch black pepper

1 large potato, in 3cm pieces
20g olive oil
700g water
2 vegetable stock cubes (p.42)

1. Preheat the oven to 200°C / 180°C Fan / Gas Mark 6.
2. Place the cauliflower florets, chickpeas and garlic cloves onto a large rectangular baking tray lined with greaseproof paper. Toss with the olive oil, cumin, paprika, salt and pepper and roast for 30 minutes until charred. Set aside.
3. Meanwhile, put the potato pieces in the mixing bowl. Chop **2 Sec. / Speed 5**. Scrape down with spatula. Add the olive oil and fry **5 Min. / 120°C / Speed 1**. Add the water and vegetable stock cubes and cook **15 Min. / 100°C / Speed 1**.
4. Once cooked, add the roasted cauliflower and chickpeas, reserving about 1 handful for garnishing, and purée **30 Sec.**, starting on **Speed 4** and gradually going all the way up to **Speed 9**.
5. Serve immediately, garnished with the reserved veggies.

Top secret tip: Freeze the soup leftovers in individual portions and thaw as needed. To reheat, simply pour into the mixing bowl and cook **10 Min. / 100°C / Speed 1**.

thai prawn soup

If you are a fan of the fragrant and refreshing flavours of Thai food, this is something that you cannot miss. The fresh veggies, prawns and coconut broth go so well together and it is the ideal soup for lunch or a light dinner.

serves
2

2 garlic cloves
1 lemongrass stalk, in 3cm pieces
30g fresh ginger, in 2cm pieces
1 shallot, halved
30g vegetable oil
400g (1 can) coconut milk
1 tsp coconut oil
400g water
1 red chilli, sliced

1 lime, zest and juice
¼ tsp rice vinegar (or white wine vinegar)
200g cooked, peeled prawns
80g cherry tomatoes
3 chestnut mushrooms, sliced
100g pak choy leaves, separated
1 pinch sea salt
5g fresh coriander

1. Place the garlic cloves, lemongrass pieces, ginger and shallot in the mixing bowl. Chop **5 Sec. / Speed 5**. Scrape down with spatula. Add the oil and fry **5 Min. / 120°C / Speed 1**.
2. Add the coconut milk, coconut oil, water, red chilli, lime zest and juice and rice vinegar and cook **4 Min. / 100°C / Speed 1**.
3. Meanwhile, put the simmering basket inside a large bowl. Pour the sauce into the simmering basket and strain the soup. Discard any bits and pour back into the mixing bowl.
4. Add the prawns, cherry tomatoes, mushrooms, pak choy and sea salt, and cook **5 Min. / 100°C / Reverse / Speed Stir**.
5. Serve hot with the fresh coriander.

I will learn: How to use the stir function to avoid chopping prawns during the cooking process

jerk chicken

Jerk chicken is my number one dinner. Jesse and I always have jerk chicken if we cannot think of anything else. This recipe is so easy and completely mess-free. I like that even before we are eating, everything is clean already. Scotch bonnet gives the jerk paste its unique flavour. If you don't like it so spicy, only use ¼ of the chilli and that is enough to make it a mild version of the hot Jamaican dish.

serves
4

30g fresh coriander, chopped
4 spring onions, in 5cm pieces
500g Greek style yoghurt
2 limes, juice only

4 chicken legs
1 Scotch bonnet chilli
30g fresh coriander
3 spring onions, in 5cm pieces
2 garlic cloves
50g fresh ginger, in 2cm pieces
20g fresh thyme
15g olive oil
40g honey

40g brown sugar
2 limes, juice only
1 tsp ground allspice
¼ tsp ground cloves
1 tsp salt
½ tsp black pepper
10g dark rum
25g cider vinegar

1 can coconut milk
650g water
250g basmati rice
1 can black beans, drained

1. Preheat the oven to 200°C / 180°C Fan / Gas Mark 6.
2. Place the coriander and spring onions in the mixing bowl. Chop **1 Sec. / Turbo / 2x**.
3. Add the Greek style yoghurt and lime juice, and combine **10 Sec. / Speed 2.5**. Pour into a small bowl and leave refrigerated until later. Rinse the mixing bowl.
4. Place the chicken legs on a large rectangular ovenproof dish lined with greaseproof paper and slice the skins with a sharp knife. This will help the sauce to be evenly distributed in the chicken.
5. Add the Scotch bonnet chilli, coriander, spring onions, garlic cloves, ginger, thyme, olive oil, honey, brown sugar, lime juice, ground allspice, ground cloves, salt, black pepper, dark rum and cider vinegar to the clean mixing bowl. Blitz **10 Sec. / Speed 10**.
6. Pour mixture over the chicken and roast in the oven for 40 minutes. Meanwhile, rinse the mixing bowl.
7. Place the coconut milk and water in the mixing bowl. Insert the simmering basket. Add the basmati rice to the simmering basket and cook **15 Min. / Varoma / Speed 1**. Add the black beans and stir into the rice with a fork. Cook again **15 Min. / 100°C / Speed 1**.
8. Serve immediately with the coriander yoghurt.

chorizo bolognese

This is my second favourite go-to recipe and we always have a batch of the delicious chorizo bolognese in our freezer ready to go for dinner. I use star anise for frying onions; it releases the most amazing aromas and flavours into the onions and can be removed later on.

serves
4–6

31 chorizo sausage (about 300g), skinned,
  in 5cm chunks
1 large onion, halved
3 garlic cloves
30g olive oil
50g butter
1 star anise
2 carrots, in 3cm pieces
2 celery sticks, in 3cm pieces
250g beef mince

1 can cherry tomatoes
1 can chopped tomatoes
100g red wine
5g dried oregano (1 Tbsp)
1 tsp sea salt
½ tsp black pepper
2 sprigs rosemary, stalks removed
1 pinch caster sugar
100g buffalo mozzarella

1. Place the pieces of chorizo in the mixing bowl. Chop **9 Sec. / Speed 9**. Pour into a small bowl and leave aside until later.
2. Place the onion and garlic cloves in the mixing bowl. Chop **3 Sec. / Speed 5**.
3. Scrape down with spatula. Add the oil, butter and star anise to the mixing bowl. Fry **10 Min. / 120°C / Speed 1**. Remove the star anise.
4. Add the carrots and celery sticks to the mixing bowl. Chop **5 Sec. / Speed 5**. Then cook **5 Min. / 120°C / Speed 1**.
5. Add the chorizo sausage and beef mince. Fry **5 Min. / 120°C / Reverse / Speed 1**.
6. Add the cherry tomatoes, chopped tomatoes, red wine, oregano, sea salt, black pepper, rosemary and caster sugar to the mixing bowl. Cook **20 Min. / 100°C / Reverse / Speed 2**. Meanwhile, cook your pasta according to the instructions on the packet.
7. Serve the pasta with the chorizo bolognese and a few pieces of buffalo mozzarella. You can freeze the leftover bolognese easily. Just divide the sauce into individual portions and place in freezer bags. Thaw as needed. Just add a fresh can of chopped tomatoes and reheat **15 Min. / 100°C/ Reverse / Speed 2**.

roast beef

Roast beef is the perfect Sunday lunch for the whole family. Served with celeriac mash and veggies, it is the ideal meal if you are really hungry and don't want to spend hours roasting meat in the oven.

serves
4

1.1 kg rolled beef roasting joint
50g red wine
2 rosemary stalks
3 garlic cloves
1 tsp sea salt
1 tsp black pepper
1000g water
2 vegetable stock cubes (p.42)
3–4 carrots, in large chunks
1 pack green beans, trimmed

20g olive oil
20g butter

1. Place the rolled beef roasting joint onto a large piece of aluminium foil. Make a little wall around it with the foil, then pour over the red wine, sprinkle with the rosemary stalks and garlic cloves and season with salt and pepper. Seal the beef in the aluminium foil and wrap tightly. Place in the Varoma.
2. Fill the mixing bowl with the water and vegetable stock cubes. Put the Varoma in place and steam 45 Min. / Varoma / Speed 1.
3. Check the beef with a Thermopen by inserting it right into the middle of the meat. It should be about 55°C so that you get a medium rare roast. If you prefer it well done, it should be 60°C–65°C. At this stage the meat will not be done yet, so it is time to add in the vegetables. Add the carrots and green beans to either side of the roast and steam again 20 Min. / Varoma / Speed 1.
4. Once cooked, transfer the vegetables onto a tray and keep warm in the oven at 100°C until ready to serve.
5. Unwrap the meat and transfer the cooking liquid from the aluminium foil into a jug.
6. Heat a large frying pan with 20g olive oil and 20g butter until sizzling hot. Seal off the roast on all sides until nicely browned. Check the temperature again; it should be 63°C for medium rare, 71°C for medium and 77°C for well done. Rest the meat on a large serving plate covered loosely with aluminium foil and a tea towel for at least 10 minutes before carving.
7. Serve with celeriac mash, vegetables and the reserved cooking liquid.

celeriac mash

This is one of the creamiest of all mash recipes. Polenta is super quick to cook and adds an amazing flavour to this wonderfully fluffy mash. You can always cook a double portion and freeze it for later.

serves
4

300g celeriac, peeled and chopped
  into 2cm cubes
¼ tsp ground cumin
20g sunflower oil
1 red onion, peeled and halved
1 celery stick, in 3cm pieces
1 vegetable stock cube (p.42)

310g water
50g polenta
½ lemon, zest
290g whole milk
1 pinch sea salt
1 pinch black pepper

1. Preheat the oven to 180°C / 160°C Fan / Gas Mark 4.
2. Place the celeriac on a large rectangular tray lined with greaseproof paper. Sprinkle with the ground cumin and 10g sunflower oil. Bake for 30 minutes.
3. Meanwhile, place the red onion in the mixing bowl and chop **3 Sec. / Speed 5**. Scrape down with spatula. Add the remaining 10g sunflower oil and fry **5 Min. / 120°C / Speed 1**.
4. Add the celery stick and chop **2 Sec. / Speed 5**. Add in the vegetable stock cube and 60g water and cook **5 Min. / 100°C / Speed 1**.
5. Pour over the remaining 250g water, polenta and lemon zest and cook **2 Min. / 100°C / Speed 1**. Then add the roasted celeriac, milk, sea salt and pepper and blitz **20 Sec. / Speed 10** until smooth. You can prepare the celeriac mash before the roast beef and reheat in the microwave just before serving.

*In this chapter you are about to discover
the wonderful world of Thermomix baking.
Enter and find out how to make your own
bread or whip up buttercream. Top tips
will help you become an artisan baker.*

....

baking

baking guide

Whisking

Insert butterfly whisk attachment. Place ingredients in the mixing bowl and whip using the settings below. For whipped cream, do not set a time, watch closely and stop when desired stiffness is achieved. Never go above speed 4 when using the whisk attachment, otherwise it may break.

	Amount	*Setting*
Double cream	300g	Watch carefully / Speed 3.5
Eggs with sugar	4 eggs, 120g caster sugar	6 Min. / 37°C / Speed 4 and another 6 Min. / Speed 4
Meringue	4 egg whites, 2 tsp cornflour (add after 40 sec.), 250g caster sugar (add spoon by spoon after cornflour) for the remaining time	4 Min. / Speed 3.5

Melting

	Amount	*Setting*
Butter	200g, small chunks	4 Min. / 50°C / Speed 2
Chocolate (e.g. dark, milk)	200g, small chunks	8 Sec. / Speed 9 then 3 Min. / 37°C / Speed 2

Milling

You can use 1 Tbsp vanilla sugar instead of ½ tsp vanilla extract in your recipe.

	Amount	*Setting*
Caster sugar	200g granulated sugar	20 Sec. / Speed 9
Chocolate	200g, small chunks	7 Sec. / Speed 9
Cinnamon sugar	200g caster sugar, 1 tsp cinnamon	10 Sec. / Speed 2
Coffee beans	200g	20 Sec. / Speed 10
Icing sugar	200g granulated sugar	
Nuts (e.g. cashew, almonds)	200g	
Seeds (e.g. sesame, poppy, sunflower)	250g	
Vanilla sugar	200g caster sugar, 1 vanilla pod	
Whole grains (e.g. wheat, rye)	250g	1 Min / Speed 10

Baking

Use the following guides to calculate cooking time in the oven, once the food is prepared.

	Amount	*Oven Setting*
Bread	1 loaf	30–40 Min. / 220°C / 200°C Fan / Gas Mark 7.
Bread rolls	6 rolls	15 Min. / 220°C / 200°C Fan / Gas Mark 7.
Cake sponge	1 large tin	25–35 Min. / 180°C / 160°C Fan / Gas Mark 4.
Cake, dense (e.g. fruit cake)		1 Hour / 160°C / 140°C Fan / Gas Mark 3.
Cookies & biscuits	12 pieces	12–15 Min. / 180°C / 160°C Fan / Gas Mark 4.
Croissants	6 croissants	20 Min. / 200°C / 180°C Fan / Gas Mark 6.
Pretzels	8 pieces	15 Min. / 220°C / 200°C Fan / Gas Mark 7.

baking basics

In this section you can read about some of the basics of baking. I have included a guide to oven temperatures, conversion from cups to grams and even my two favourite basic sponge recipes: chocolate sponge and vanilla sponge.

guide to oven temperatures

I use a fan oven at home and base all my recipes on that. If you have a different oven, make sure to use the below guide to oven temperatures to find out which temperature to go for.

Electricity °C	Electricity (fan) °C	Gas Mark
110	90	¼
120	100	½
140	120	1
150	130	2
160	140	3
180	160	4
190	170	5
200	180	6
220	200	7
230	210	8
240–250	220–230	9

converting cups to grams

If you are living in a country which usually relies on cups rather than grams, you may wonder how to convert some of your favourite recipes into the right measures. I have listed the most important cake and baking ingredients in this section, which will help you determine your quantities.

It is important never to mix both measures, i.e. using grams and cups in one recipe. It will get very confusing and you may end up with the wrong consistency. Always stick to one or the other for best results.

Butter

Cups	Grams
¼ cup	57 g
½ cup	113 g
¾ cup	170 g
1 cup	227 g

Plain & strong white flour, icing sugar	
Cups	Grams
¼ cup	32 g
½ cup	64 g
¾ cup	96 g
1 cup	128 g

Caster sugar, granulated sugar	
Cups	Grams
¼ cup	50 g
½ cup	100 g
¾ cup	150 g
1 cup	200 g

basic sponge cakes

These are my favourite basic sponge cake recipes. You can use the vanilla sponge with buttercream and jam to make a Victoria sandwich or the chocolate sponge to make a Black Forest gateau. Both are perfect bases for making beautiful creations.

vanilla sponge

4 eggs
225g caster sugar
225g plain flour
225g butter
1 tsp vanilla extract
1 Tbsp baking powder

chocolate sponge

4 eggs
245g caster sugar
225g plain flour
225g butter
1 tsp vanilla extract
1 Tbsp baking powder
40g cocoa powder
30g boiling water
2 Tbsp rum

Method

1. Preheat the oven to 180°C.
2. Place the eggs, caster sugar, plain flour, butter, vanilla extract and baking powder in the mixing bowl. Combine **30 Sec. / Speed 5**. While mixing, insert your spatula through the mixing bowl lid and stir to help make a smoother batter.
3. If you are making the chocolate sponge, combine the cocoa powder with the boiling water and rum in a small bowl and combine with a fork until you have a thick batter. If it is too thick, add a bit more boiling water.
4. Add to the batter in the mixing bowl and combine again **10 Sec. / Speed 5**.
5. Pour into two 20cm cake tins and bake for 25–30 minutes. Remove and leave to cool on a wire cooling rack.

top secret tips

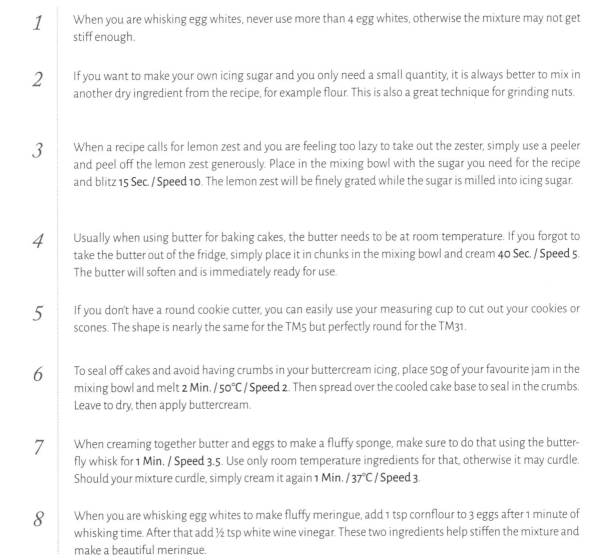

1 When you are whisking egg whites, never use more than 4 egg whites, otherwise the mixture may not get stiff enough.

2 If you want to make your own icing sugar and you only need a small quantity, it is always better to mix in another dry ingredient from the recipe, for example flour. This is also a great technique for grinding nuts.

3 When a recipe calls for lemon zest and you are feeling too lazy to take out the zester, simply use a peeler and peel off the lemon zest generously. Place in the mixing bowl with the sugar you need for the recipe and blitz **15 Sec. / Speed 10**. The lemon zest will be finely grated while the sugar is milled into icing sugar.

4 Usually when using butter for baking cakes, the butter needs to be at room temperature. If you forgot to take the butter out of the fridge, simply place it in chunks in the mixing bowl and cream **40 Sec. / Speed 5**. The butter will soften and is immediately ready for use.

5 If you don't have a round cookie cutter, you can easily use your measuring cup to cut out your cookies or scones. The shape is nearly the same for the TM5 but perfectly round for the TM31.

6 To seal off cakes and avoid having crumbs in your buttercream icing, place 50g of your favourite jam in the mixing bowl and melt **2 Min. / 50°C / Speed 2**. Then spread over the cooled cake base to seal in the crumbs. Leave to dry, then apply buttercream.

7 When creaming together butter and eggs to make a fluffy sponge, make sure to do that using the butterfly whisk for **1 Min. / Speed 3.5**. Use only room temperature ingredients for that, otherwise it may curdle. Should your mixture curdle, simply cream it again **1 Min. / 37°C / Speed 3**.

8 When you are whisking egg whites to make fluffy meringue, add 1 tsp cornflour to 3 eggs after 1 minute of whisking time. After that add ½ tsp white wine vinegar. These two ingredients help stiffen the mixture and make a beautiful meringue.

9   If you are whisking double cream to make lovely whipped cream in the Thermi and you forgot to pay attention, do not worry. You can simply turn that overwhipped mixture into butter. Find the recipe for that on p.50.

10   Tempering chocolate is much easier using the Thermomix than with any other kitchen gadget. The simplest trick is to place the chocolate chunks in the mixing bowl and blitz **7 Sec. / Speed 9** to break it up into small crumbs. Then you can melt the chocolate more easily. The recommended temperature is always no higher than 37°C, otherwise the chocolate may separate and you end up with an oily mess.

baking bread

'Let the steam out'

Making our own bread in the Thermomix is a big achievement for most of us. The first time I made a successful bread with my Thermi was a day of celebration. The feeling that I don't have to go out and buy bread whenever I run out and that I can fill the whole house with this gorgeous smell just makes me proud. There are a few basics that you need to keep in mind, so read on and find out what you can do to make the perfect loaf of bread.

ingredients

Baking with the right ingredients makes a big difference to the quality of your bread. The key determinants are the yeast you use, the flour and the order of ingredients.

yeast

You can choose between fresh yeast and dried yeast. All my recipes are based on dried yeast. If you wish, you can replace 1 Tbsp dried yeast with 30g fresh yeast. Alternatively, if you are using dried yeast, look out for one that states 'quick yeast' or 'instant yeast'. It is the best one to use because it activates quicker than the other types of dry yeast. You can also buy 'dry active yeast' or 'fast acting yeast', which may be slightly slower to rise, so make sure you keep an eye on your dough.

flour

To make bread, the best flour to use is strong white bread flour. Plain flour is weaker and made from softer wheat, which is therefore lower in gluten and protein. For an elastic bread dough you need high protein and gluten contents to get a smoother dough that holds its shape well while baking. Alternatively, you can also use rye, spelt, buckwheat or wholemeal flour. These types of flour are richer and therefore sometimes might be slightly stickier or take longer to be incorporated into a dough.

gluten free flour

When baking with gluten free flour, remember that the dough is not going to come together like a standard dough. When using gluten free flour you will get a thick cake batter consistency that you need to pour straight into a tin and leave to rise there. The best way to use gluten free flour is to go for a ready-mixed blend for best results.

kneading and proving

Kneading times for dough will depend on the types of flour you use to make your loaf of bread. For white dough made of strong white bread flour, kneading times are around 2 minutes, whereas darker flours and doughs containing whole grains take about 3 minutes. Brioche takes about 10 minutes because you need to ensure you incorporate the butter properly into the dough. It is important to knead the dough long enough to activate the gluten and produce enough elasticity.

Proving time varies according to the flour used. For white flour, the proving time is much shorter than for darker flours, such as rye flour. If you don't want to wait all day before baking your bread, you can always wrap your dough in cling film or place it in an oiled bowl covered with cling film. Refrigerate overnight so that the dough can rise slowly and start fermenting. Take out the next day and leave to come to room temperature for 30 minutes before baking.

top tips

1. To remove dough easily from the mixing bowl, tip the bowl upside down onto a lightly floured surface. Remove the cap, then press down the blade so that it goes inside. Lift up the bowl and remove the blade. To remove the leftover dough residue, put the mixing bowl back together and spin on Turbo 2x. This should force all the dough against the walls of the mixing bowl and it will be easy to remove with a spatula.

2. It is vital to always activate yeast in the mixing bowl first by warming it with the liquid you use for the recipe, such as water or milk. Warm **2 Min. / 37°C / Speed 2**.

3. To achieve a lovely crust, brush your baguette with a mixture of water and ½ tsp salt just before baking. The salt will react while baking and make the baguette much tastier.

4. Use the measuring cup to cut out bread rolls from dough. Then you can brush each bread roll with a bit of water and dip it into some seeds before baking.

5. When milling whole grains, make sure only to use 250g at a time and mill **1 Min. / Speed 10**. To mill it more coarsely, reduce the time for milling to **40 Sec. / Speed 10**.

the butterfly whisk

'Whisk it up'

The butterfly whisk is by far my favourite element of the Thermomix. It is such a neat little tool and so powerful. The first thing to note is to never use it above speed 4 as it can break. You can make the most wonderfully fluffy sauces, meringue and buttercream with the butterfly whisk. I use it almost every day.

did you know?

If you are making a creamy sauce, it helps to insert the butterfly whisk and fluff it up for **40 Sec. / Speed 4** at the end of cooking to beat some air into the sauce and make it much creamier. This little trick is especially helpful for making Hollandaise sauce, Béarnaise sauce or a lemon sauce for fish. Use the butterfly whisk to make a stiff meringue. The trick to the best meringue is to play with the speed a bit. I tend to increase the speed from 3.5 to 4 in the last 20 seconds to make the mixture very stiff and get the best meringue.

To decorate your cake, you can use the butterfly whisk to make the fluffiest, no-curdle buttercream. The key is not to heat it for too long, so follow the recipes below for the best results. Another thing that your butterfly whisk does really well is zabaglione, which is one of my favourite desserts. It is a fluffy combination of eggs and champagne or white wine and is like eating a cloud. It melts in your mouth and the whisk makes it so incredibly airy, you feel like you are hardly eating anything.

Buttercream icing	Place 250g butter in small chunks in the mixing bowl. Blitz **40 Sec. / Speed 5**. Scrape down with spatula, then insert the butterfly whisk. Whisk **2.5 Min. / Speed 3.5**. While whisking, slowly add in 500g icing sugar through the mixing bowl lid a spoonful at a time. At the end, add a splash of water through the lid and you are ready to use the buttercream. You can add in any food colouring right at the end or even a splash of your favourite curd or alcohol.
Coconut cream icing	Insert the butterfly whisk. Place 1 can of chilled coconut cream (not milk) in the mixing bowl. Whisk **1.5 Min. / Speed 3.5**. While whisking, slowly add in 200g icing sugar through the mixing bowl lid a spoonful at a time. At the end, add ¼ tsp xanthan gum. Then chill until needed.

my baking routine

Baking is my life. Even more than cooking, I bake to relax and I bake to unwind. It is what I grew up with and what I love to do. Baking with Thermomix is just another step towards ultimate efficiency. I learned how to bake when I was little, so it has always been a big part of me and I truly noticed that practice makes perfect. After batches and batches of funny looking cookies, I finally figured out how to make them. It takes time to be really good at baking but you can produce some wonderful results on the way.

I have included a collection of my favourite baking recipes in this book and most of them are so simple to prepare, I would say that they are even child friendly. There was hardly anything I didn't try when I was young, so there is no harm in getting the kids involved and letting them experiment with ingredients and flavours.

Sunday afternoon was our traditional teatime in Germany and I have brought some of that tradition over to London. Jesse and I usually make a cake on Sunday or at least have something sweet I have baked previously with our tea. Two of my absolute favourites are mini Victoria sponge (p.148) and for those of us with a really sweet tooth it is raspberry chocolate tart (p.160). When I get asked what my favourite thing to bake is, I always think about something special but all I can say is, I am a fan of simplicity. I didn't call my blog tag-line 'baking made simple' for nothing. My number one recipe is marble cake and I have so many memories attached to this cake, I don't think anything will ever compete with that. Recently I discovered the crumble topping for marble cake and made a really nice recipe for you to try (p.151), and that has got to be the one for me. Apart from that, my whole family is obsessed with it and every birthday we have a marble cake on the table.

There are a few things that I always make sure of when baking. Before starting with any batter mixing or dough kneading, make sure your oven is preheated. It will make baking so much easier and reduce baking times. You also end up with an even bake that gives you a much better result. I also always have a bamboo or wooden skewer at hand to test whether my cakes are fully baked. I insert it into the middle of the cake all the way through and pull it back out to see whether any batter sticks to it. If not, the cake is fully baked.

A baker is nothing without the right tools. I only use round springform cake tins for baking and anodised loose-bottom flan tins for pies and tarts. These are the best baking tins out there and very easy to handle. They don't have to be expensive. Just make sure that they are non-stick.

fluffy dinner rolls

If you haven't discovered the wonders of Thermomix bread yet, this is the recipe to start with. These super fluffy, soft dinner rolls are perfect for dipping into soups, as burger buns or with some pulled pork. You can make the dough the evening before and refrigerate overnight, or in the morning and refrigerate until the evening. Simply take it out of the fridge 30 minutes before you are ready, let it warm a bit and continue with the recipe. These are perfect rolls for freezing as well.

makes
6

225g water
75g milk + extra for brushing
1 Tbsp dry active yeast
500g strong white bread flour
  + extra for dusting

1 tsp salt
30g butter, in small chunks
10g caster sugar

1. Place the water, milk and dry active yeast in the mixing bowl. Warm **2 Min. / 37°C / Speed 2**.
2. Add strong white bread flour, salt, butter and sugar and knead **2 Min. / Kneading function**.
3. Leave to prove for 1 hour, then tip onto a lightly floured surface. To remove from the bowl easily, tip the bowl upside down. Remove the base, then press down the blade so that it drops down inside. Lift up the bowl and remove the blade from the dough.
4. Cut the dough into 6 equal pieces using a dough scraper or your Thermi spatula. Roll each piece into a ball and place onto a large baking tray lined with greaseproof paper. Leave a 3cm gap in between each bread roll.
5. Cover with a tea towel and leave to rise for another 30 minutes.
6. Meanwhile, preheat the oven to 220°C / 200°C Fan / Gas Mark 7.
7. Uncover the rolls and brush with some milk. Bake for 15–20 minutes until golden. The rolls should sound hollow when tapped.

I will learn: — How to use the kneading function to make easy bread rolls
— My spatula can cut the dough with the sharp edge and makes portioning simple

poppyseed bloomer

Everyone always dreams of making their own bread at home but quickly decides it involves too much work and they will never do it as well as the bakery. I would say, you just haven't made the right bread yet. This super fluffy poppyseed bloomer loaf is so amazing and fluffy, it is almost as if you are eating a cloud. And it is so simple to prepare. It does not require much work with your hands and you can also freeze half the bread once baked. Thaw as needed and bake for 5 minutes in the oven at 200°C to make it fresh again.

makes
1 large
loaf

450g water
2 Tbsp dry active yeast
750g strong white bread flour
2 tsp salt

10g olive oil
20g poppy seeds
3–4 ice cubes

1. Place the water and yeast in the mixing bowl and warm **2 Min. / 37°C / Speed 2**.
2. Add in the strong white bread flour, salt and olive oil and knead **2 Min. / Kneading function**.
3. Leave to rise in the mixing bowl for 1 hour, until doubled in size. Preheat the oven to 250°C / 230°C Fan / Gas Mark 9.
4. To remove the dough from the bowl, tip the bowl upside down onto a lightly floured surface. Remove the base, then press the blade down so that it drops down inside. Lift up the bowl and remove the blade from the dough.
5. Spread the dough into a large rectangle about 3cm thick and 30cm long. Fold the two ends in about 4cm and then roll up the dough lengthways starting with the long end closest to you. This will ensure you have a tight roll that will hold its shape when baking.
6. Carefully lift onto a baking tray lined with greaseproof paper and brush the top with some lukewarm water. Sprinkle with the poppy seeds and, with a sharp serrated knife, score the bread 4 times in a very quick movement.
7. Cover for another 10 minutes, then place in the oven. Put the ice cubes in the bottom of the oven, close the door and leave to bake for 10 minutes. Then turn down the oven to 200°C and bake for another 20–25 minutes until it sounds hollow when tapped.
8. Remove from the oven and leave to cool on a wire cooling rack.

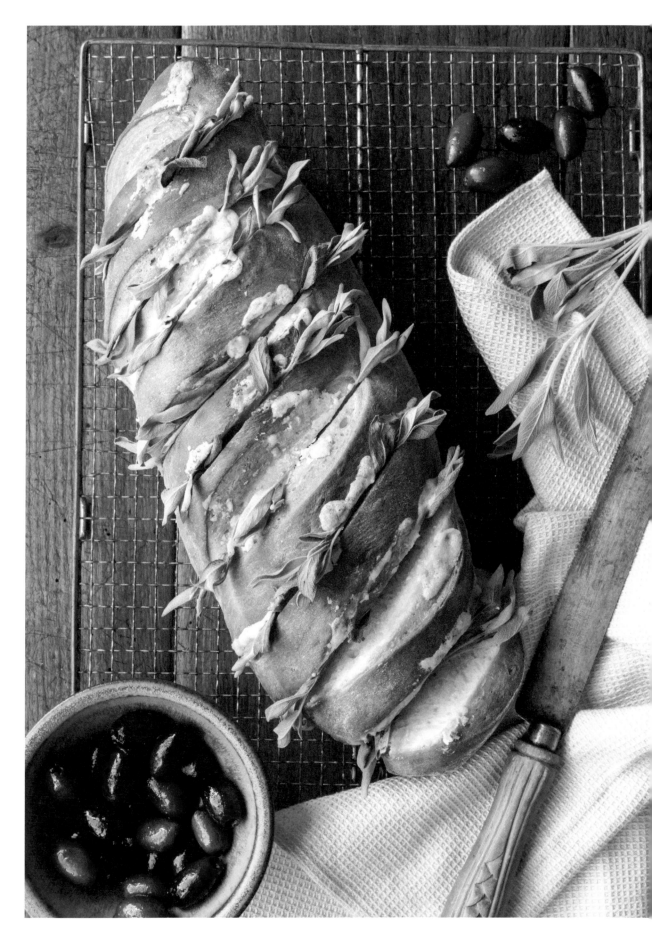

sage garlic bread

This is the most wonderful tear and share bread, ideal for a lazy evening on the sofa with some nibbles and a glass of wine. You can also add ham to make it more of a meal, although the bread is already lovely without the filling and makes a great sandwich base.

makes
12 slices

2 garlic cloves
300g water
1½ Tbsp dry active yeast
500g strong white bread flour
  + extra for dusting
20g olive oil
1½ tsp salt

10g caster sugar
3–4 ice cubes
75g Cheddar cheese
3 garlic cloves
30g butter
20g fresh sage leaves

1. Place the garlic cloves in the mixing bowl. Blitz **5 Sec. / Speed 5**.
2. Add the water and yeast and warm **2 Min. / 37°C / Speed 2**.
3. Add the strong white bread flour, olive oil, salt and caster sugar and knead **2 Min. / Kneading function**.
4. Leave to rise for 1 hour in the mixing bowl with the lid on, until doubled in size. Alternatively, you can place the dough on a piece of greaseproof paper and wrap in cling film. Chill overnight.
5. Once risen (or chilled), preheat the oven to 250°C / 230°C Fan / Gas Mark 9.
6. Place the dough on a lightly floured surface. Press into a large rectangular shape, using your hands. It should be about 25cm long and 3cm thick. Roll up into a large log, starting with the edge closest to you. Place onto a large rectangular tray lined with greaseproof paper.
7. Score with a sharp serrated knife in a quick movement, then cover and leave for another 10 minutes.
8. Remove the cover and place in the oven. Add the ice cubes to the bottom of the oven and bake for 20–25 minutes, until it sounds hollow when tapped. Leave to cool for at least 30 minutes. You can at this stage use the bread as it is or continue making the garlic and sage filling.
9. In a clean mixing bowl, place the Cheddar and garlic cloves. Blitz **5 Sec. / Speed 9**. Scrape down with spatula. Add the butter and combine **5 Sec. / Speed 5**.
10. Cut slits in the bread and smear some of the garlic butter in each slit, decorating it with some sage leaves.
11. Place on a baking tray lined with greaseproof paper and bake for another 5–7 minutes until the cheese has melted.

quinoa chia bread

This is one of my favourite vegan and gluten free breads. The technique is very simple and the bread does not require any kneading. You simply need to soak the seeds overnight so that they are nice and soft for the baking day. The bread does not last very long, so it is best to store it in a bread bag in a cool and dry place.

makes
1 loaf

120g chia seeds
340g quinoa
500g water

60g olive oil
1 tsp bicarbonate of soda
10g maple syrup
1 lemon, juice
½ tsp salt
50g water
30g mixed seeds

1. The evening before, soak the chia seeds and quinoa in the water by placing them in a small bowl, covering it with cling film and refrigerating it overnight.
2. The next day, when you are ready to make the bread, preheat the oven to 160°C / 140°C Fan / Gas Mark 3.
3. Place 350g of the soaked quinoa / chia seed mixture in the mixing bowl. Add the olive oil, bicarbonate of soda, maple syrup, lemon juice and salt and blitz **15 Sec. / Speed 10**. Scrape down with spatula.
4. Add the remaining soaked quinoa chia seed mix and water and combine **1 Min. / Speed 7**.
5. Pour the mixture into a 1-pound loaf tin, sprinkle with the mixed seeds and bake in the oven for 70 minutes. Remove and leave to cool entirely on a wire cooling rack. It will firm up as it cools, so wait before cutting it.

pitta bread

Pitta bread makes the most amazing dipping tool. I use it to dip into cacik (p.80) and you can make really tasty pitta bread chips with these lovely flatbreads. They are super easy to prepare and don't require much work with your hands. In the oven, the pitta breads develop lovely air pockets which makes them even more fluffy and flakey. You can freeze them after baking and thaw as needed – simply bake in the oven for 5 minutes at 200°C to refresh them.

basic recipe

makes
4–6

150g water
1 Tbsp dry active yeast
250g strong white bread flour

10g nigella seeds
1 tsp salt
5g olive oil

1. Place the water and dry active yeast in the mixing bowl. Warm **2 Min. / 37°C / Speed 2**.
2. Add the strong white bread flour, nigella seeds, salt and olive oil and knead **2 Min. / Kneading Function**.
3. Preheat the oven to 250°C / 230°C Fan / Gas Mark 9. Put a large rectangular tray in the oven to warm up.
4. Leave the dough to rise for 30 minutes, then tip onto a lightly floured surface. To remove from the bowl easily, tip the bowl upside down. Remove the base, then press down the blade so that it drops down inside. Lift up the bowl and remove the blade from the dough.
5. Cut the dough into 4–6 equal pieces using a dough scraper or your Thermi spatula. Roll each piece out to an oval and place on a piece of greaseproof paper that fits the tray in the oven. You may need 2 pieces.
6. Remove the tray from the oven, place the piece of greaseproof paper with bread on it, bake for 10–15 minutes until puffed up but still quite light and place on a wire cooling rack to cool slightly covered with a tea towel.

pitta bread chips

makes
4–6

3 pitta breads
10g olive oil
1 tsp sea salt flakes

½ tsp black pepper
½ tsp smoked paprika
½ tsp garlic powder

1. Preheat the oven to 200°C.
2. Cut the pitta breads into small pieces and place on a baking tray lined with greaseproof paper. Drizzle with the olive oil, then sprinkle over the sea salt flakes, black pepper, smoked paprika and garlic powder.
3. Bake for 10–15 minutes until crispy and dark brown.

pretzel hot dogs

How nice is the combination of pretzel and hot dog? These super tasty pretzel hot dogs are pure comfort food. After a long day, this is the best thing you can make for the whole family. I personally love pretzels and paired with sausage and sauerkraut it makes such an unusual combination. The buns can be frozen as well.

makes
6

300g whole milk
1½ Tbsp dry active yeast
30g butter
500g strong white bread flour
1½ tsp salt
10g caster sugar

1000g water
1 Tbsp bicarbonate of soda
1 tsp sea salt flakes
6 frankfurters
100g sauerkraut
Ketchup or mustard as needed

1. Place the whole milk and dry active yeast in the mixing bowl. Warm **2 Min. / 37°C / Speed 2**.
2. Add the butter, strong white bread flour, salt and caster sugar and knead **2 Min. / Kneading Function**.
3. To remove the dough from the bowl easily, tip the bowl upside down onto a piece of cling film. Remove the base, then press down the blade so that it drops down inside. Lift up the bowl and remove the blade from the dough. Form the dough into a square and cover with cling film. Refrigerate overnight, or if you want to make pretzel hot dogs for dinner, make the dough in the morning and refrigerate while you are at work or doing errands in the day.
4. After it has risen, remove the dough from the fridge and unwrap. Divide the dough into 6 equal pieces widthways using a dough cutter or your spatula. Roll each piece into a long sausage shape and place seam side down on a large rectangular tray lined with greaseproof paper. Make sure to leave 4cm gaps in between each bun. Cover with a tea towel and leave to rise for 45 minutes.
5. Preheat the oven to 220°C / 200°C Fan / Gas Mark 7.
6. Meanwhile, heat the water with the bicarbonate of soda in a large saucepan. When boiling, dip each bun in the hot water and simmer for 30 seconds. Remove with a ladle and place back on the tray. Sprinkle with salt and repeat with the rest.
7. Bake for 25 minutes until golden brown. Remove and leave to cool on a wire cooling rack.
8. Serve with hot frankfurters and sauerkraut.

pizza fakeout

Before you grab the phone to order takeaway, read this recipe for the most delicious pizza. It makes an ideal family activity and you can involve everyone with the toppings and get creative. I absolutely adore pizza night and at home we all had our hands in the pizza dough, helping dad. You can freeze the pizza by taking it out of the oven just before it is baked and freeze. Bake from frozen for another 10 minutes.

serves
4–6

300g water
1 Tbsp dry active yeast
500g strong white bread flour

1 tsp salt
20g olive oil

1. Place the water and dry active yeast in the mixing bowl. Warm **2 Min. / 37°C / Speed 2.**
2. Add the strong white bread flour, salt and olive oil and knead **2 Min. / Kneading function.** Leave to rise in the bowl for 1 hour until doubled in size.
3. Preheat the oven to 250°C / 230°C Fan / Gas Mark 9.
4. To remove the dough from the bowl easily, tip the bowl upside down onto a lightly floured surface. Remove the base, then press down the blade so that it drops down inside. Lift up the bowl and remove the blade from the dough.
5. Divide the dough into 2 equal pieces using a dough cutter or spatula. Roll each out into a large circle. Place on a baking tray lined with greaseproof paper and prick the base of the pizza with a fork, top with any toppings you like, then bake in the oven for 20 minutes until crispy and golden.

spinach and egg topping:
3 Tbsp tomato passata
1 tsp dried oregano

1 handful fresh spinach
20g grated mozzarella
1 egg

6. Place all toppings except for the egg on the pizza, starting with the tomato passata and oregano. Bake for 15–20 minutes; after 10 minutes, crack the egg on top and leave until crispy golden and the egg is baked through.

Top secret tip: — You can easily make this a spelt or wholemeal pizza by replacing the strong white bread flour and following the steps as stated in the recipe. The dough may be a bit tougher, so add a bit of water to make it slightly smoother and easier to work with. If it is sticky, use some semolina or polenta on the work surface to remove any moisture.
— Use 00 flour if it is available in your country. It makes the pizza dough much smoother and super fluffy.

parmesan rosemary shortbread

What a lovely treat to come home to. Freshly baked savoury shortbread with some cheese and wine. The perfect end to a successful day. Parmesan and rosemary make a perfect flavour combination for a biscuit. These little discs of pleasure are perfect for dipping into cacik (p.80) and are perfect for freezing. You can prepare the discs and freeze them individually. Thaw as needed.

makes
20–24

80g Parmesan cheese, in small chunks
1–2 sprigs fresh rosemary, stalks removed
1 garlic clove
225g plain flour

1 tsp sea salt
150g butter
20–30g water

1. Preheat the oven to 180°C / 160°C Fan / Gas Mark 4.
2. Place the Parmesan, rosemary and garlic clove in the mixing bowl. Blitz **8 Sec. / Speed 9**. Remove 1 Tbsp and set aside in a small bowl.
3. Add the plain flour, sea salt and butter and mix **20 Sec. / Speed 6**. While mixing, add some water through the lid until the mixture comes together like a coarse pastry.
4. Place the dough on a piece of cling film and form into a long log. Refrigerate for 1 hour. At this stage you can also freeze the log and defrost it when you need it.
5. Cut into 2cm pieces and place on a baking tray lined with a large piece of greaseproof paper. Sprinkle the individual shortbreads with a bit of the reserved cheese mixture and bake for 10–12 minutes until light brown.
6. Remove and leave to cool on a wire cooling rack. They will harden as they cool.

Top secret tip: This recipe makes a wonderful savoury tart shell as well and you can, instead of shaping the dough into a log, just shape into a disc, refrigerate or freeze and use to line a tart base.

berry scones

In Britain, there is no afternoon tea without scones. These super berry scones are the perfect twist on the original and if you are tight for time, they are ideal to prepare in a hurry. Serve with some fresh clotted cream and strawberry jam.

makes
6

250g plain flour
1 pinch salt
50g golden caster sugar
100g buttermilk
1 Tbsp baking powder
1 egg

50g butter
30g raspberries
30g blueberries

Clotted cream
Strawberry jam (p.30)

1. Preheat the oven to 220°C / 200°C Fan / Gas Mark 7.
2. Place the plain flour, salt, golden caster sugar, buttermilk, baking powder, egg and butter in the mixing bowl. Mix **20 Sec. / Speed 6**.
3. Remove the dough from the mixing bowl and place on a floured surface. Roll out to 3cm thickness and cut out rounds using a 6cm cookie cutter or your measuring cup.
4. Place on a baking tray lined with greaseproof paper and decorate with a few blueberries and raspberries. Press them in slightly so that they don't fall off while baking.
5. Bake for 10–15 minutes until lightly golden and puffed up. Leave to cool on a wire cooling rack, then serve with some clotted cream and jam.

I will learn: How to mix ingredients in the Thermomix so that they comes together as a smooth dough

blueberry cookies

These blueberry cookies are the perfect vegan snacks in between meals. They are packed with protein and you can easily freeze them and thaw as needed. You can either use almond or peanut butter to make these delicious cookies. When they come out of the oven they are very soft so make sure to leave them to harden before you eat them.

makes
12–15

150g gluten free oats
90g olive oil
120g agave nectar
160g crunchy almond or peanut butter
90g tahini

½ tsp vanilla extract
½ tsp sea salt
½ tsp bicarbonate of soda
100g buckwheat flour
150g blueberries

1. Preheat the oven to 180°C / 160°C Fan / Gas Mark 4.
2. Line two large rectangular trays with greaseproof paper.
3. Place the oats in the mixing bowl and blend **3 Sec. / Speed 10**. Place into a small bowl until later.
4. Add the olive oil, agave nectar, almond butter, tahini and vanilla extract to the mixing bowl. Warm **2 Min. / 40°C / Speed 2**.
5. Pour in the reserved oats, sea salt, bicarbonate of soda, buckwheat flour and blueberries and mix **20 Sec. / Reverse / Speed 2**.
6. Spoon tablespoonfuls of the mixture onto the prepared trays with at least 4cm gaps in between. Round them slightly with your fingers, press down to make a nice cookie shape and bake for 10–12 minutes.
7. Remove and leave to cool on the trays until hardened, then transfer onto a cooling rack and leave to cool entirely.

F

mini victoria sponge

Victoria Sponge is the queen of all cakes. I didn't discover it until I came to the UK and I immediately fell in love with it. This one is a mini version of the original and I have designed it to be super quick and simple to prepare. The buttercream takes less than 3 minutes and the sponge itself is ready in 30 seconds. It doesn't get much quicker than that.

makes
3

225g caster sugar
225g plain flour
225g butter
4 eggs
1 tsp baking powder

½ tsp vanilla extract
1 quantity buttercream (p.126)
100g strawberry or raspberry jam
   (see recipe on p.30 or use store-bought)
20g icing sugar

1. Preheat the oven to 180°C / 160°C Fan / Gas Mark 4.
2. Line two 20cm springform cake tins with greaseproof paper. Place aside.
3. For the cake, place the caster sugar, plain flour, butter, eggs, baking powder and vanilla extract in the mixing bowl. Combine **30 Sec. / Speed 5**.
4. Divide the cake mixture between the two tins and bake each for 25–30 minutes until golden brown. Place on a wire cooling rack to cool.
5. Once cool, use a 10cm cookie cutter or a glass the same size and cut out 6 rounds from your prepared cakes. Place aside.
6. Divide the buttercream between 3 of the cake rounds, top with some jam and sandwich with the other cake bases. Dust with some icing sugar and serve.

Top secret tip: To freeze the cake, simply place it in the freezer and thaw as needed. The cake is also super tasty as a frozen cake in the summer.

marble crumble cake

Whenever I get asked about my signature bake, I always answer with one thing: marble crumble cake. This is a great twist on the classic. I have added a crumble topping and my god it is so tasty. Such a good cake and perfect for afternoon tea.

makes
16 slices

topping:
50g butter
100g golden caster sugar
150g plain flour

cake:
300g butter
250g caster sugar
1 tsp vanilla extract
1 pinch salt
5 eggs
370g plain flour
1 Tbsp baking powder
70g whole milk
30g cocoa powder
200g dark chocolate chips

1. Preheat the oven to 180°C / 160°C Fan / Gas Mark 4.
2. Line a 24cm round springform cake tin with greaseproof paper.
3. For the crumble topping, place the butter, golden caster sugar and plain flour in the mixing bowl. Blitz **20 Sec. / Speed 6**. While mixing, slowly add a little water until the mixture resembles fine crumbs. It will be dry at this stage but do not worry. Place in a separate bowl until later.
4. For the cake, place the butter in the mixing bowl. Blitz **40 Sec. / Speed 5**. Add the caster sugar, vanilla extract, salt, eggs, plain flour, baking powder and 40g whole milk and combine **40 Sec. / Speed 5** while stirring with spatula through hole in mixing bowl lid and helping the batter come together.
5. Pour half the cake batter into the prepared tin, distributing it evenly. Leave the rest in the mixing bowl.
6. Add the cocoa powder and remaining 30g whole milk and combine **5 Sec. / Speed 5**. Scrape down with spatula and repeat **5 Sec. / Speed 5**. Pour over the vanilla batter in the tin and using a fork in a circular motion fold in the chocolate mixture. You don't want to marble it too much, just a few folds with the fork.
7. Press the crumble together with your hand and sprinkle it over the cake batter. Decorate with the dark chocolate chips and bake for 55–60 minutes.
8. Remove, place on a wire rack and allow to cool.

gin & tonic cake

This gin & tonic cake is a mixture of a lemon drizzle cake and a gin & tonic on a plate. My boyfriend Jesse is completely obsessed with gin and since I am not such a big fan of it, I thought, why not try it in a cake and the results are absolutely beautiful. Next time, I might just try having a real G&T on the side.

makes
12 slices

200g butter
200g caster sugar
4 eggs
75g Greek style yoghurt
275g plain flour
30g gin
2 lemons, zest and juice
1 tsp vanilla extract
1 Tbsp baking powder

5 lemons, juice only
2 lemons, sliced
130g golden caster sugar
10 juniper berries
50g tonic water
20g gin

1. Preheat the oven to 180°C / 160°C Fan / Gas Mark 4.
2. Place the butter, caster sugar, eggs, Greek style yoghurt, plain flour, gin, lemon zest and juice, vanilla extract and baking powder in the mixing bowl. Combine **30 Sec. / Speed 5.**
3. Pour into a 2-pound loaf tin lined with greaseproof paper. Bake in the oven for 45–55 minutes until golden brown and a skewer comes out clean.
4. Meanwhile, to make the syrup, place the lemon juice, lemon slices, golden caster sugar, juniper berries and tonic water in a large non-stick frying pan. Heat until bubbling. Leave to bubble for 5 minutes, then remove from the heat and stir in the gin.
5. Poke a few holes in the warm cake with a wooden skewer. Drizzle the syrup over the cake and decorate with the juniper berries and lemon slices.

redcurrant pie

Pie, oh pie. Almost better than apple pie is my all-time favourite, redcurrant pie. It keeps so well in the fridge and is one of the most refreshing pies ever. It's a perfect dessert for the whole family and, if you want, you can serve it with fresh vanilla ice cream to make it the ultimate pleasure.

makes
16 slices

200g plain flour
1 tsp baking powder
100g butter
75g caster sugar
1 egg

400g redcurrants
1 Tbsp cornflour

3 eggs, separated
50g caster sugar
200g double cream
40g cornflour
½ tsp vanilla extract

1 tsp cornflour
150g icing sugar

1. Place the plain flour, baking powder, butter, caster sugar and egg in the mixing bowl. Mix **20 Sec. / Speed 6**. Remove the pastry and wrap in cling film. Chill for 30 minutes.
2. Meanwhile, preheat the oven to 180°C / 160°C Fan / Gas Mark 4. Clean the mixing bowl.
3. In a small bowl, combine the redcurrants with the cornflour and set aside.
4. Remove the dough from the fridge, unwrap and roll out to a thick circle that fits inside a 24cm loose-bottomed pie dish. Make sure to cover the edges of the dish and prick the bottom with a fork. Pour the redcurrants into the base of the tin.
5. To make the filling, separate the eggs. Keep the whites aside and place the yolks in the mixing bowl. Add the caster sugar, double cream, cornflour and vanilla extract and mix **10 Sec. / Speed 5**. Pour over the redcurrants and bake for 30–35 minutes.
6. Meanwhile, insert the butterfly whisk into the clean mixing bowl. Add in the leftover egg whites and whisk **3 Min. / Speed 3.5**. After 1 minute, add the cornflour through the lid while the blade is still running. After a further 20 seconds, slowly add the icing sugar through the lid teaspoon by teaspoon, waiting in between teaspoons for at least 5–10 seconds. In the last 20 seconds, increase the speed to 4.
7. Remove the pie from the oven, spread the meringue over it and return to bake for another 12–15 minutes.
8. Remove and leave to cool on a wire rack before serving.

orange polenta cake

Being gluten free means that often you cannot enjoy all the lovely pastries and cakes that everyone makes. But this super tasty orange polenta cake is the perfect alternative not only if you are allergic to gluten but also if you are vegan. It is so delicious and the cashew cream is the perfect topping.

makes
16 slices

200g cashews
300g water
110g agave nectar
½ orange, zest and juice
½ tsp orange extract
5g coconut oil
50g water
120g polenta
80g ground almonds

100g gram flour
1 Tbsp baking powder
2 oranges, juice and zest
100g olive oil
100g agave nectar
½ tsp orange extract
100g soya yoghurt

100g crushed pistachios

1. Soak the cashews for 4 hours in the water. Drain and place in the mixing bowl.
2. Add the agave nectar, orange zest and juice, orange extract, coconut oil and water and blitz **1 Min. / Speed 10**. Pour into a small container and refrigerate until later.
3. Preheat the oven to 180°C / 160°C Fan / Gas Mark 4. Line an 18cm round springform cake tin with greaseproof paper.
4. Place the polenta, ground almonds, gram flour, baking powder and orange zest in the mixing bowl. Blitz **10 Sec. / Speed 10**. Add the orange juice, olive oil, agave nectar, orange extract and soya yoghurt and combine **30 Sec. / Speed 4**.
5. Pour into the prepared tin and bake for 30–35 minutes until golden brown and a skewer inserted into the cake comes out clean.
6. Place on a wire rack until cool. Then decorate with the cashew cream and sprinkle with some crushed pistachios.

apple blackberry traybake

When I was young we had an apple tree at home. During the apple season we used to go out and pick apples from the tree and make the most delicious apple cake. At the same time the blackberries were also in season and one year we created this super tasty apple blackberry traybake.

makes
24 slices

250g butter
250g caster sugar
250g plain flour
1 tsp vanilla extract
1 Tbsp baking powder
4 eggs
½ tsp ground cinnamon

3 Braeburn apples
200g blackberries

1. Preheat the oven to 180°C / 160°C Fan / Gas Mark 4.
2. Place the butter, caster sugar, plain flour, vanilla extract, baking powder, eggs and ground cinnamon in the mixing bowl. Mix **40 Sec. / Speed 5**.
3. Core the apples and slice into 1cm thick pieces.
4. Place half the batter into a 20cm square cake tin lined with greaseproof paper and smooth out. Scatter half the apple rings over the batter, cover with the other half of the batter, decorate with the remaining apple rings and sprinkle the blackberries on top.
5. Bake in the oven for 30–40 minutes until golden brown and fluffy. Remove and leave to cool on a wire rack.

raspberry chocolate tart

I must admit, I have a weakness for chocolate and also raspberries. Anything pink really. This super delicious raspberry chocolate tart is the perfect dessert. You can prepare it in advance and leave it in the fridge for up to three days.

makes
16 slices

150g plain flour
3 egg yolks
50g caster sugar
1 pinch salt
75g butter
½ tsp vanilla extract

300g dark chocolate
300g double cream
200g fresh raspberries

1. Preheat the oven to 180°C / 160°C Fan / Gas Mark 4.
2. Place the plain flour, egg yolks, caster sugar, salt, butter and vanilla extract in the mixing bowl. Mix **20 Sec. / Speed 6**. Wrap the pastry in cling film and chill for 30 minutes.
3. Remove from the cling film and place on a floured surface. Roll out to fit a 22cm tart dish. Line the tart dish with the pastry, prick with a fork and place a sheet of greaseproof paper on top. Fill with baking beans and blind bake for 15 minutes.
4. Remove the baking beans and greaseproof paper and bake again for another 6–8 minutes at 160°C / 140°C Fan / Gas Mark 3 until baked all the way through. Remove and leave to cool down on a wire rack.
5. To make the ganache, place the dark chocolate in the mixing bowl. Chop **7 Sec. / Speed 9**. Scrape down with spatula. Add the double cream and melt **4 Min. / 37°C / Speed 3**.
6. Place the raspberries in the bottom of the tart shell and pour over the ganache. Leave to set for at least 2 hours before serving.

apricot caramel pavlova

Once you master the art of making your own meringue in the Thermomix, you will never go back. This is a great dessert to make for the whole family. The meringue is made with nuts and the salted caramel sauce is perfect for serving with lots of desserts.

serves
6–8

500g apricots, pitted and halved
3 pieces stem ginger in syrup, finely sliced
  + 2 Tbsp syrup
20g golden caster sugar

100g hazelnuts
250g golden caster sugar
2 tsp cornflour
2 tsp white wine vinegar
6 egg whites
500g Greek style yoghurt

1. Preheat the oven to 220°C / 200°C Fan / Gas Mark 7.
2. Place the apricot halves on a large rectangular tray lined with greaseproof paper. Scatter over the stem ginger pieces, syrup and golden caster sugar and roast for 15 minutes.
3. Place the hazelnuts on a roasting tray and roast for 5–7 minutes. Tip into the mixing bowl and blitz **2 Sec. / Speed 5**. Pour into a small bowl and leave to cool.
4. Turn the oven down to 180°C.
5. Place a small bowl on top of the mixing bowl. Weigh in the sugar and place aside.
6. Clean the mixing bowl vigorously. Insert the butterfly whisk. Place 3 egg whites in the mixing bowl. Whisk **3 Min. / Speed 3.5**. After 1 minute, add 1 tsp cornflour and 1 tsp white wine vinegar through the lid while the blade is running. After a further 20 seconds, slowly add half of the golden caster sugar through the lid teaspoon by teaspoon, waiting in between teaspoons for at least 5 seconds. In the last 20 seconds, increase the speed to 4. Pour the mixture into a large bowl and set aside.
7. Clean the mixing bowl vigorously and repeat step 6 with the other half of the egg whites, cornflour, white wine vinegar and golden caster sugar. Add that mixture to the first bowl of meringue and add the hazelnuts. Gently fold them in with the spatula and pour onto a large rectangular baking tray lined with greaseproof paper.
8. Flatten the middle and leave the edges slightly higher. Bake for 45 minutes until golden brown. Leave to cool, then spread over the Greek style yoghurt and decorate with the apricots. Spoon over some salted caramel sauce and serve.

caramel
sauce:

120g butter
200g brown sugar
80g double cream
½ tsp sea salt flakes

Place the butter, brown sugar, double cream and sea salt flakes in the mixing bowl. Cook **10.5 Min. / Varoma / Speed 3 / no measuring cup**. Pour into a sterilised jar and keep in the fridge for up to 1 month. Before serving, you can reheat in the mixing bowl **2 Min. / 50°C / Speed 2**.

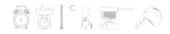

In this chapter you will learn the best tricks for cleaning your Thermomix. Find out how to clean leftover chocolate from the bowl and many more top secret tips.

cleaning

Top Secret Tips

....

Well-deserved Drink

top secret tips

1   The self-clean function of the Thermomix is one of the key features that you always need to keep in mind. Every time you are finished using the mixing bowl, add a little drop of washing up liquid and fill the bowl with 1l water. Pulse on **2x / Turbo** then rinse. If you have a lot of dirt, instead of pulsing it, self-clean it **60 Sec. / 60°C / Speed 6**. Rinse and you are ready to go again.

2   You can buy a set of spout brushes which is perfect for cleaning the Thermomix. The smaller brush is ideal for cleaning all the nooks and crannies of the blade. The brushes can also be put in the dishwasher to clean.

3   If you have a bit of a smelly mixing bowl from the last food you have cooked and you are about to make yourself a drink or something sweet, simply take some whole coffee beans and grind **20 Sec. / Speed 10**. Coffee is known to neutralise smells and will help you get a much better-smelling mixing bowl. Rinse afterwards with some washing up liquid.

4   Another great trick to get rid of odours on your Thermomix lid, if you don't have coffee beans to hand, is to make a thick paste of bicarbonate of soda and water in a small bowl. Spread it on the inside of the lid and leave for 15 minutes to soak, then rinse well with washing up liquid. To do the same for the mixing bowl, add 2 tsp bicarbonate of soda and the juice of 1 lemon to the mixing bowl. Heat **15 Min. / Varoma / Speed 3** and rinse afterwards with washing up liquid.

5   When you have been very busy frying onions or making sauces in the Thermi, you can sometimes get some burning on the bottom of the mixing bowl. To get rid of those residues, you can either use steel wool to scrape it off or simply place 1 lemon, halved, in the mixing bowl. Blitz **5 Sec. / Speed 10**, then scrape down and add 350g water. Cook **10 Min. / Varoma / Speed 3**. Rinse the mixing bowl and the burned bits should come off easily with a larger cleaning brush or scourer.

6   Sometimes your Thermi just needs a thorough clean. For that, add 750g water, 250g vinegar (I use white wine vinegar, but any light vinegar will do), 2 Tbsp bicarbonate of soda and heat **15 Min. / Varoma / Speed 3**. Rinse with washing up liquid and voila, you have a super shiny mixing bowl.

7   When the mixing bowl is discoloured after you have made a curry or fried some onions and given it a purple tinge, this usually occurs because of residue from oil. You can use a simple trick with lemon. The best thing to do is to add the juice of 1 lemon, 350g water and 1 tsp bicarbonate of soda to the mixing bowl. Clean **10 Min. / Varoma / Speed 3**. Then rinse with washing up liquid and leave to stand in the sunlight for 20 minutes to dry.

8   For a stained lid after cooking with turmeric, you can utilise sunlight. Simply rub half a lemon on the lid and leave in the sun for at least 1 hour. You can easily place it by a sunny window and just leave it there, then rinse with dishwasher liquid and you have a clean lid again. The lemon juice almost acts like a vegan bleach for tough discolourations.

9   When you have dough residue underneath your blade, you can simply add some egg shell and 200g water to the mixing bowl and a few splashes of washing up liquid. Blitz **3–4x / Turbo** and you can get even the toughest dough residue out. Afterwards, rinse with washing up liquid.

10   One of my all time favourite tricks is the towel drying trick. To dry your mixing bowl, simply pop a tea towel into the mixing bowl and mix **15 Sec. / Reverse / Speed 2**.

peach wine slushies

Phew, that was a lot of recipes, tips and tricks. I am sure you have already become an expert at using your Thermomix. But for now, after all that practice, you deserve a drink. So make this super-lovely Peach wine slushy and enjoy. Have some well deserved me-time.

makes 2

3 ripe peaches, halved and pitted
300g white wine
4–5 ice cubes

1. Place the peaches, white wine and ice cubes in the mixing bowl. Blitz **1 Min. / Speed 10**. Serve immediately and enjoy.

index

acknowledgements

First and foremost, I would like to thank Jesse, the absolute best partner, for being so supportive and motivating me to finally take a leap of faith into the unknown world of self-employment. Without you and your countless night shifts, I would have never been able to get to this stage. From the very first day, you have always believed in my work and the things that I do and given me strength in moments of doubt. You are my rock and I cannot wait to explore many more book writing adventures with you.

Of course, I would like to express my deepest gratitude to my parents, Manfred and Inge, or Mämmchen and Päppchen as I call them, for giving me the starting point and foundation of business knowledge. I have been so lucky to learn from two such experienced entrepreneurs, and without your knowledge of numbers, suppliers and many other business wisdoms I don't think I would be here today. My wonderful mum, who I was lucky enough to have visit me in the busiest time during the book making process, has helped me with cleaning, preparing, taking pictures, holding equipment at all angles and positions, and has just been there to fully support me on a bad day. And my wonderful dad has always given me some extra baking advice when I had a total disaster. He is my favourite baker.

I would also really like to thank Felicity Knight who has taken on the very important job of proofreading all my work. You made sure that all my dashes were the right length and all the sentences actually made sense. You have such an incredible eye for detail and I am very happy to have found someone so thorough to make this book a great success.

A huge thank you to all my other friends who have kindly looked at my book to ensure it doesn't contain any funny English or backwards sentences. Thank you Chris, Ben and Gill.

Want more?

If you have got a taste for the delicious recipes I can offer for Thermomix, head over to my online shop at www.thermomixbakingblogger.com/shop and purchase a copy of my fabulous baking book *Homebaked: ThermoMix.Bake.Eat.Repeat* for more amazing recipes for the TM5 and TM31. All the accessories I have used in this book, such as nut milk bags, dough scrapers, bread proofing baskets, etc., can be found in my shop.

www.thermomixbakingblogger.com/shop